Collaborative Lesson Study

ReVisioning Teacher Professional Development

Vicki S. Collet

Foreword by Ellin Oliver Keene

TEACHERS COLLEGE PRESS

TEACHERS COLLEGE | COLUMBIA UNIVERSITY

NEW YORK AND LONDON

Published by Teachers College Press, 1234 Amsterdam Avenue, New York, NY 10027

Copyright © 2019 by Teachers College, Columbia University

Cover design by Holly Grundon / BHG Graphics. Cover photo by saknakorn / iStock by Getty Images.

Library of Congress Cataloging-in-Publication Data can be found at loc.gov..

ISBN 978-0-8077-6307-0 (paper)
ISBN 978-0-8077-6308-7 (hardcover)
ISBN 978-0-8077-7806-7 (ebook)

Printed on acid-free paper
Manufactured in the United States of America

This book is dedicated to all who have learned with me through the Lesson Study process. Thank you for opening your schools, your classrooms, and your minds.

Contents

Foreword

Coincidentally, I am writing this Foreword for Vicki Collet's lovely book as I fly 35,000 feet over her home in Arkansas. I did look down to wave, but I don't think she waved back. She was probably observing in a classroom surrounded by colleagues and students, taking notes at a furious pace and imagining the debriefing discussion to come. Or, she may have been huddled around a table in a teachers' lounge debriefing that lesson, considering each teacher's insights from the lesson and thoughts about what lies ahead in their own classrooms. As I flew over, Vicki was probably immersed in Lesson Study, one of the most potent known approaches to teacher professional learning, one that empowers teachers to explore problems of practice, reflect deeply upon their instruction, posit new approaches, and pose questions about student learning—again and again. It is a practice based on "relentless curiosity" about children and modifying our practices to better serve them.

As Vicki points out, we don't have an English word that refers simultaneously to both teaching and learning. Japan, where lesson study was pioneered, does have such a word. *Oshieru*. We know that complex ideas are often caged in the paucity of words we use to define and describe them. This is especially true for the synchronous, interdependent process that is teaching and learning. Oshieru. I think it's a concept we ought to consider carefully and adopt. Oshieru—teaching and learning including professional learning—involves reciprocal processes shaped by the context in which they happen. As Vicki points out, in order to improve student learning, engender joy and engagement for children, and continually improve our practice, we need to consider teaching and learning as interdependent and occurring in a particular context—in your particular context. What is the drive behind that process? Wonder. Questions. Complexity. Confusion. All of the above, but especially collaboration.

Lesson Study asks us, as teachers, to collaborate, to a degree that is, perhaps, unprecedented in our experience. It asks that we move beyond our instinct to close our classroom doors and teach as we always have. It asks that we are vulnerable and share with our colleagues the problems of practice we all face. This process asks that we open our classrooms to colleagues and—good, bad, or ugly—lean in to study what we find there.

In *Collaborative Lesson Study*, Vicki Collet provides the ultimate guide to this extraordinarily valuable process. This book is infinitely practical, yet refuses to provide "canned" lessons and rigid rules about how teachers must approach curriculum. Vicki acknowledges the importance of educational research and values the resources we teachers have but insists—in my view correctly—that we are the decisionmakers and that the best professional learning is bottom up—coming from those closest to the kids—rather than top down. She emphasizes that "as you and your colleagues participate in Lesson Study, you create a community of experts. You become the expert on what works in your classrooms with your students. After reviewing what others have said about strategies for teaching your content, you will plan with your colleagues for instruction that meets your students' needs." These ideas just make sense!

I don't have a favorite chapter, but if I did it, would have to be Chapter 8 on Flexibility. Collet's thinking about the critical need for flexibility during lesson design and implementation is particularly incisive and will clarify when and how we make in-the-moment decisions based on observing students and responding to their needs. She honors teachers' judgment, offers us affirmation for the times when we deviate from the lesson design, and suggests that those deviations provide fodder for extremely productive discussion following the lesson.

I love nothing more than a great question about teaching and learning, and Lesson Study is founded on great questions that often lead to other questions. *Collaborative Lesson Study* provides the path to the most meaningful professional learning many of us will experience, and I, for one, am deeply grateful to Vicki for writing this significant book.

—Ellin Oliver Keene
May 2019

Introduction

> We have an education system that is always reforming, but not always improving.
>
> —James Hiebert, in Hanford (2015)

The field of education seems to be in perpetual motion, shifting from reform to reform (Bryk, Gomez, Grunow, & LeMahieu, 2015). In an effort to find the "fix" for problems in today's schools, policy and practice are often imposed from above on teachers and students whose culture and context are not considered in the decisionmaking process. This leads to ill-fitting solutions that restrict the agency of those with the potential to make the greatest change—the teachers who know and understand the needs and interests of the students in their classes.

This book, instead, presents a process called Lesson Study that will guide you to re*Vision* your own practice in ways that make sense culturally and contextually for you and your students. It is work that I have taken up with teachers of preschool through college, from urban and rural contexts, and across academic content areas. I have seen the ability of Lesson Study to empower teachers as they respond to the varied needs of learners. As you read about Lesson Study and hear stories of empowerment and improvement, I hope you'll be inspired to take up this work. I invite you to join me in an ongoing quest that values teachers and teaching, learners and learning.

Lesson Study is as straightforward as it sounds: the study of a lesson. However, Catherine Lewis, who learned about Lesson Study in Japan and has been instrumental in spreading its use in the United States, points out that during Lesson Study

> [Teachers] improve the lessons not as an end in itself, but as a way to deepen their own content knowledge, their knowledge of student thinking, their understanding of teaching and learning, and their commitment to improvement of their own practice and that of colleagues. . . . Lesson study is not about discovering the one right way to teach a lesson, but about building knowledge of many teaching strategies and habits of observation, inquiry, and analysis of practice. (Lewis & Hurd, 2011, p. 24)

The goal of Lesson Study is not to create the ideal lesson that is universally useful. Whether you are a preservice or inservice teacher, you have doubtless been taught and encouraged to use "best practices." Although it is true that some practices are more effective than others (and research has much to teach us), it is also true that there is no single, perfect lesson. This is true because you and I, and the students we teach, are diverse in so many ways. Lesson Study focuses on "the why of teaching: why teaching methods work in particular ways in particular settings" (Smagorinsky, as cited in Garcia & O'Donnell-Allen, 2015, p. 5). The Lesson Study process of collaborative planning, teaching, and objective observation leads to lesson revision that is guided by insights gained. Let me show you how that played out in a 5th-grade class in a high-poverty school where I worked with teachers using the process.

LESSON STUDY IN A TURNAROUND SCHOOL

Right after I had concluded a districtwide training for elementary teachers, I was approached by Linda, an energetic 5th-grade teacher who came to me with determination and mildly muted anger. She pointed repeatedly at a page in the notebook in her hand. "Here's what we're doing," she said. "We are really good teachers; we are working really hard. I just need you to tell me if we're doing the right thing. I don't want them to come at the end of the year and say, 'You were doing this all wrong.'" The "them" whose retribution Linda feared was district personnel, who had targeted teachers at Linda's "Turnaround" school because of low test scores. Unfortunately, as the district's literacy coordinator, I was one of "them." What could I do to relieve the pressure and increase the performance at Linda's high-needs school?

I began by arranging a meeting with the 5th-grade team. When Linda and her colleagues Kim and Allie joined me around the long table in their conference room at Parker Elementary School, tension was thick in the air. Anger bubbled up as they described "meetings, meetings, meetings" that were "stealing time from students." They wanted someone to do something, not just call more meetings. I also sensed that they wanted someone to shift the blame to: "Tell us what to do and we'll do it," they said. This implied that if it didn't work, at least it wouldn't be their fault. Getting the district to give them a plan was their defense against blame. Teachers' feelings of efficacy had deteriorated in the face of high-stakes accountability. By the end of the meeting, I had committed to help. Lesson Study became the answer that transformed not only their students' writing, but also their efficacy in a context of tension and high-stakes accountability.

AN OVERVIEW OF LESSON STUDY

In contrast to top-down reforms, Lesson Study is professional development that empowers teachers to drive improvement as they determine new ideas and methods to incorporate into their teaching. This job-embedded professional learning process has the potential to improve student achievement by looking closely at classroom practice. Throughout this book, you'll read how Lesson Study helped Linda, Kim, and Allie (and many other teachers) do just that.

The overarching goals of Lesson Study are to build pathways that enable continual growth of the knowledge, interpersonal resources, and motivation required to improve teaching and learning. Teachers' agency is honored, and their efficacy increases as they design and witness ever-improving cycles of instruction. For the 5th-grade team at Parker Elementary, that meant giving them the permission they felt they needed to break away from strictly following a purchased curriculum and figure out what worked for their kids. Instead of sticking like glue to the teachers' guide, we drew from many resources, looked at research, and, most important, made adjustments based on how lessons played out with their students. None of the teachers' guides or materials they'd collected from trainings could anticipate responses of the unique blend of students at Parker, where 80% of students qualified for free or reduced-price lunch, 59% were students of color, 26% were English language learners (ELLs), and 9% had been designated as having special education needs. Teachers needed an approach that drew on knowledge in the field about effective instruction but was responsive to their students' needs and interests. Lesson Study encouraged this flexibility.

Lesson Study is bottom-up professional development. It starts with what teachers know and can already do, and it can be applied across the educational spectrum. Although Lesson Study has its origins in Japanese elementary education, it was brought to the United States in 1998 by Catherine Lewis (Lewis & Tsuchida, 1998). Since that time, Lesson Study has been used in enclaves across the nation that have documented success in improving teaching and learning. Our Lesson Study at Parker focused on writing instruction, but Lesson Study is utilized in a variety of academic areas and across grade levels (Hurd & Licciardo-Musso, 2005; Marble, 2007; Pesick, 2005).

Implementing Lesson Study

As you participate in Lesson Study, you will collaboratively plan lessons that become the focus of inquiry on effective teaching practices. Then you'll observe one another teach lessons and collaboratively revise and refine your instructional plans, as illustrated in the vignette below.

At Parker Elementary, the 5th-grade team started their Lesson Study during a unit on expository writing. Students were writing reports about animals and had gathered information on note cards and digital files. One of the first tasks the teachers and I undertook was to plan a lesson that would help students figure out how to organize the facts they had collected into a logical sequence for their report. We looked at suggestions for teaching organization from several teachers' guides and decided that students would work in groups, each with a set of sentence strips that was an expository text cut apart. Kim had some ideas about texts she could use, so she volunteered to teach first. The rest of us observed, taking feverish notes about student thinking.

Kim's introduction to the activity was brief. She told her students the task and let them go. No modeling, no hints about what to look for, no chart to guide the activity. I watched students struggle even with the process of how to manage group-work and tried to hold my skepticism at bay. Giving Kim the benefit of the doubt, that she knew her students and knew what she was doing, I watched the lesson unfold. From initial chaos, students eventually worked together to reconstruct paragraphs and papers. It was a messy, impactful learning process.

During our debrief that afternoon, Linda said, "I could never do that. I'd have a hard time changing to try it this way." Allie added, "I want to hold my kids' hands and have them do it **my** way." Alice, their special education colleague who joined us for some of the meetings, pushed, "But they need to learn how to overlay an organization." Alice talked about the complicated home lives many students led, with multiple caregivers as parents worked several jobs, and how students navigated their own roles in this process. "They need to know that they can make order," she said. Kim affirmed, "I try to be really careful not to overscaffold. They didn't really need a procedure for organizing. We do them a disservice if we don't make them think." The reasoning and explanations that Alice and Kim provided won the point, and we all learned a lesson about overscaffolding. This discussion helped us strengthen the lesson in ways that were responsive to students' experiences and needs and make revisions that Linda and Allie put to use when they taught the lesson the next day.

Our experience with this lesson on organization in expository writing demonstrates the Lesson Study cycle, as illustrated in Figure I.1. We started by studying resources; we created a plan for the lesson and observed while Kim taught it. Together, we reflected on how the lesson had unfolded and the student learning that had occurred. These insights helped us re*Vision* the lesson. For example, our experience looking closely at student thinking gave us new views about the level of scaffolding that was appropriate. Finally, Linda and Allie had the opportunity to reteach this revised lesson the following day.

The Lesson Study process supported Allie, Kim, and Linda as they designed instruction that was responsive to their context. It supported their students as they got instruction that met their needs. Lesson Study is a conceptually simple but powerful process for instructional improvement that benefits both teachers and students.

Figure I.1. The Lesson Study Cycle

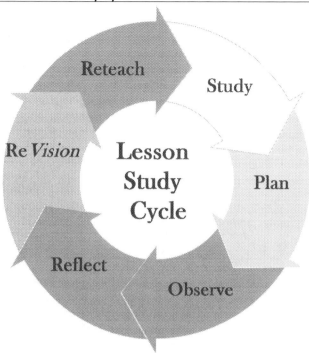

Observation to Re*Vision* Practice

Observation is the cornerstone of effective Lesson Study. In the writing lesson described above, having five pairs of teacher eyes helped us zero in on what students knew and were able to do. Through careful observation of both teachers and students, we were able to recognize effective and less effective practices.

Opening classroom doors for peer observation might feel risky at first. Typically, the expectations in American classrooms are similar to a vacation phrase I'll co-opt: "What happens in my classroom, stays in my classroom." However, during Lesson Study teachers come to perceive postobservation feedback not as a personal evaluation, but rather as an opportunity for instructional improvement. This happens because the lessons that are observed are collaborative products of the Lesson Study process.

As French novelist Marcel Proust (1974) astutely recognized, "The real voyage of discovery consists not in seeking new landscapes, but in having new eyes" (p. 131). Lesson Study encourages teachers to see classroom interactions with new eyes. Teachers who have carefully researched and crafted a lesson bring critical eyes to the classroom. While observing a research lesson, you will be attuned to nuances of both teacher moves and student response. Your careful observation and thoughtful reflection will go beyond simply revising lessons. Through Lesson Study, you can re*Vision* instruction.

Although research lessons are ideally drawn from cohesive units, the Lesson Study process brings laserlike attention to single lessons. The lesson becomes a microcosm for understanding instructional practices that can then be broadly applied. By looking closely at one lesson, you'll be able to identify techniques that can be used in many situations. For example, by recognizing the benefits of co-creating anchor charts with students during a lesson on making inferences, elementary teachers may recognize the general utility of this practice and begin using anchor charts during math lessons. Lesson Study is not just about improving the single lesson; it is about improving the overall teaching/learning process in ways that are both generic and sensitive to the unique needs of learners.

In addition to elevating effective practices, Lesson Study also provides a window for considering students' progress toward long-term learning goals. As you acquire "the eyes to see children" (Lewis, Perry, & Murata, 2006, p. 7)—or students of any age—you'll recognize how students are developing, individually and as a learning community. You will look closely at what children are learning, identify their misconceptions, and design ways to address them. Attention to individual students improves learning for all students. Lesson Study supports improvement that is adapted to local contexts while increasing teachers' pedagogical and content knowledge, developing professional learning communities, and increasing teachers' motivation and efficacy (Bieda, Cavanna, & Ji, 2015; Bocala, 2015; Honigsfeld & Cohan, 2008; Lewis & Perry, 2014; Lewis, Perry, Friedkin, & Roth, 2012; Marble, 2007; Perry & Lewis, 2009; Puchner & Taylor, 2006; Sibbald, 2009).

IMPACT OF LESSON STUDY ON STUDENT LEARNING

In addition to improving instruction, a growing base of research evidence demonstrates the impact of Lesson Study on student achievement (Collet, 2017; Dudley, 2012; Gersten, Taylor, Keys, Rolfhus, & Newman-Gonchar, 2014; Lewis, Perry, Hurd, & O'Connell, 2006). Gerstein and colleagues' review of research on professional development in the United States considered 643 studies on approaches to improving math teaching. They evaluated impact using the stringent criteria of the U.S. government's What Works Clearinghouse (https://ies.ed.gov/ncee/wwc/). Of the approaches studied, only two were found to have positive effects on students' math achievement; one of them was Lesson Study. Similarly, effective results were shown when underachieving schools in the United Kingdom adopted Lesson Study. In these schools, the average increase in results in English and mathematics statutory tests of 11-year-olds in schools using Lesson Study increased at double the rate of schools not provided with this support (Dudley, 2012).

The impact of Lesson Study on student learning is demonstrated in a study of a California school that used Lesson Study schoolwide. This school showed statistically significant increases in math achievement on the state test when compared with results from the district and state. The 3-year net increase on the state standardized test for students who remained at the schoolwide Lesson Study site was more than triple that of students who remained at other district schools (91 vs. 26 scale score points, F =.309, df = 845,p < .001) (Lewis et al., 2006).

Similarly, my own experience with Lesson Study at the "Turnaround" school described above demonstrates the impact on students' writing achievement. Fifth-grade students' growth percentile on the state writing test went from the 39th to the 52nd percentile, and within-group change (from students' 4th- to 5th-grade assessment) went from the 25th percentile to the 52nd percentile. These changes were significant in that they helped move the school from the "Turnaround" to the "Performance" category (surpassing the two categories—"Priority Improvement" and "Improvement"—that are in between).

What made these impressive changes in student achievement possible? My experience suggests that success rests on the shared responsibility teachers take through Lesson Study, on teachers' focus on redesigning practice, and on the power teachers are given to respond to the specific needs of their students. In my study at the Turnaround school, teachers moved from feeling an external locus of control (No matter what I do, I can't win; this is outside of my control) to an internal locus of control (What I do makes a difference!). There were tensions and challenges along the way as these shifts occurred, but the agency and empowerment teachers felt gave them the grit they needed to persist in the difficult process. As Angela Duckworth (2016) points out in *Grit: The Power of Passion and Perseverance*, "There are no shortcuts to excellence. Developing real expertise, figuring out really hard problems, it all takes time" (p. 54). Lesson Study is not a quick fix. It is a cycle for instructional improvement that pays ongoing dividends.

ABOUT THIS BOOK

My goal with Collaborative Lesson Study is to enable teachers to oppose educational reform efforts that minimize teacher agency by giving them a research-based tool for improving teaching and learning that starts in their own classrooms. Lesson Study supports teachers as instructional decisionmakers who are responsive to their students' needs, knowledge, and culture. This is important in the United States, where the diversity of students requires consideration of context and culture. Increased attention to rurality and ongoing attention to urban issues highlight the importance of context when considering instructional best practices. What is "best practice" in one context is not in another, and Lesson Study allows for and encourages these distinctions through a focus on student response during observations. The varied cultural composition of our classrooms deserves similar attention. The guiding principles in this book, along with the protocols and templates provided, make Lesson Study an exceptional tool for ensuring that instruction is contextually and culturally responsive.

Because classrooms and schools are complex, this book does not supply lessons that can be lifted and used "as is" in the classroom. Instead, the book provides recommendations for developing and maintaining a stance of flexibility and responsiveness, recognizing that teaching is improvable, but not perfectible. I offer structures for attending to students' cultures, interests, knowledge, and values when planning, teaching, reflecting, and revising instruction. The Lesson Study cycle expounded in this book creates a climate for ongoing growth and re*Visioning* of practice that values teaching and teachers, learning and students. During Lesson Study, schools are places of learning for both students and teachers.

Re*Visioning* is for preservice or inservice teachers interested in improving their teaching practice. It is for professional learning communities working together to increase student learning. And it is for instructional leaders, whether in the classroom or out, who want to bring this process to their team, school, or district. Upcoming chapters of this book provide examples of Lesson Study in action and guidance for engaging in the Lesson Study cycle in your own work. At the end of each chapter, the Reflect and Respond feature provides additional resources and opportunities to mull over what you've read about.

Collaborative Lesson Study is divided into three parts. Part I contrasts Lesson Study with other forms of professional development, demonstrating Lesson Study as contextualized professional learning that counters scripted instruction and is responsive to students' needs. The chapters in this part focus on developing a mindset that is open to the uncertainty and risk necessary for meaningful change.

Part II takes an analytic look at the layers of the Lesson Study process. This part can guide you as you undertake your first Lesson Study cycle. Included are chapters centered on collaborative planning, objective observation, and reflection that lead to re*Visioning*.

Part III takes the thinking and learning of Lesson Study deeper. Once you have experienced the Lesson Study cycle, the chapters in this part will guide you to deeper consideration of the goals of building understanding, instructional flexibility, and teaching in ways that are contextually and culturally responsive.

The Conclusion of this book includes further considerations for teachers' ongoing use of the Lesson Study process. In this chapter, I revisit benefits of Lesson Study as an ongoing process for instructional improvement.

Through the pages of this book, you'll experience Lesson Study with teachers in schools from urban, suburban, and rural parts of our country spanning the spectrum from kindergarten to high school. Some of these teachers are veterans; others are preparing to enter the profession. Each teacher's experience offers insight about the work we are doing as professionals to address the needs of our students.

James Surowiecki, in his book *The Wisdom of Crowds* (2005), says, "Under the right circumstances, groups are remarkably intelligent and are often smarter than the smartest people in them" (p. xiii). As you read and appropriate the practices described in this book, my hope is that you will create and sustain remarkably intelligent groups of teachers who re*Vision* their work to create stronger teaching and learning.

Videos of Lesson Study meetings and other materials to support Lesson Study are available at VickiCollet.com.

NOTE

In gratitude to teachers who have participated in Lesson Study, I've used their real names in the book whenever possible. Any teachers' names mentioned in conjunction with Old Wire Elementary, Stilwell High, or Berryville Public Schools are real names (although students' names have been changed). For those at "Parker Elementary School," pseudonyms are used because of research requirements, but you know who you are, and I thank you!

PART I

LESSON STUDY AS RESPONSIVE PROFESSIONAL LEARNING

CHAPTER 1

Engaging in Lesson Study
Risk-Taking, Resilience, and Re*Visioning*

Instruction is a two-sided coin: When we think about instruction, we must consider both the teacher and the learner. The Japanese language has a single word that describes the teaching/learning process: *oshieru*. Similarly, Russians speak of teaching/learning with a single verb: *obuchenie*. Even though a single word for this process is absent from the English language, to effectively re*Vision* instruction, we must consider both aspects of the process. What the teacher does certainly influences the students, and the reciprocal should also be true. Given this assumption, how could we expect a scripted program to provide appropriate instruction? How could we expect canned professional development, often delivered by an outside "expert," to positively impact teaching and learning?

Short-term workshops are unlikely to influence practice or improve student achievement. Billions of dollars have been spent on professional development in the United States, with a trend toward less effective, shorter-duration trainings (Blank, de las Alas, & Smith, 2008; Wei, Darling-Hammond, & Adamson, 2010; Yoon, Duncan, Lee, Scarloss, & Shapley, 2007). As noted by Michael Fullan (2007), an educational reform leader, externally imposed professional development is not "powerful enough, specific enough, or sustained enough" to effect lasting change (p. 35).

Real changes in instructional practice and student learning come about through professional development that is focused at the classroom level. As suggested by Thomas Guskey (2005), "The hard lesson we have gleaned from analyzing various waves of education reform is that it doesn't matter what happens at the national, state, or even district level. Unless change takes place at the building and classroom levels, improvement is unlikely" (p. 40). No matter the grand imperatives and high-level planning, it is in the classroom where changes in teaching and learning can actually occur, so it makes sense to start there.

Lesson Study is located in the classroom. It focuses on student learning and addresses methods of teaching specific content. Because Lesson Study is a highly collaborative process, it builds strong working relationships among teachers. It is intensive, ongoing work that includes feedback and reflection. It is not surprising, then, that research is finding Lesson Study to be a highly effective process for teacher learning. These very characteristics have been identified by research as principles for designing powerful professional development (Darling-Hammond, Hyler, & Gardner, 2017; Horn & Little, 2010; Johnson & Fargo, 2014; Marrongelle, Sztajn, & Smith, 2013; Whitcomb, Borko, & Liston, 2009).

As you and your colleagues participate in Lesson Study, you create a community of experts. You become the expert on what works in your classrooms with your students. After reviewing what others have said about strategies for teaching your content, you will plan with your colleagues for instruction that meets your students' needs. Your careful observation and analysis of your students' learning will provoke your own learning.

This is what happened for Kim, Linda, and Allie, the 5th-grade team I worked with at Parker Elementary. After focusing on helping students organize their writing, as described in the Introduction, we next turned our attention to how students could include more "juicy details" in the animal reports they were preparing. We had noticed that when reading about their animals, students often gasped with surprise and shared interesting facts they were learning with their friends seated close by. But these tantalizing tidbits weren't making it into their own reports. Somewhere in the reading–note-taking–writing process, the very things that made the animals interesting to them were disappearing. What was happening, and how could teachers prevent the escape of interesting information as students wrote their reports? We pondered this together as we planned a lesson on details.

During our planning session, the teachers read an article about using mentor texts to improve student writing (Buckner, n.d.), and we decided to use excerpts from students' reading anthology and from *National Geographic* as examples. We would help students figure out what worked for these authors, and then students would write vivid details about their animals on sticky notes and stick them on their desks. Then the class would do a silent gallery walk around the room, reading all the sticky notes and voting on their favorite vivid details. Staying quiet would encourage students to make their own judgments, we felt, and would keep students focused during the task. Allie volunteered to teach the lesson first.

During the lesson observation, Allie taught while the rest of us watched carefully for student responses. We took notes about what students were doing and saying. While Allie read aloud the excerpts we had selected from the student anthology and *National Geographic* magazines, we noticed that students were active listeners. As the passages were read, students responded first about the content of the passages and then later, with Allie's prompting, they talked about the craft authors had used when describing their animals. Students talked about how the unusual facts that authors included got their attention. We noticed how students dug into their notes when Allie asked them to look for similarly interesting details about their animals, and we saw that Allie circulated among students as they jotted these descriptions on sticky notes. During the silent gallery walk, we noted students' enthusiasm about sharing their own findings. We saw heads nodding and fingers pointing as students silently campaigned for their own or others' details. Students cast their votes with a simple checkmark on their favorite sticky note. When Allie put the "winning" detail under the document camera, we noticed that students talked about specific words they liked.

After school, when we got together to talk about the lesson, we wondered together about the connection between juicy details and word choice, and this discussion helped us make revisions that strengthened the lesson. We decided that focusing on the specific words used in the mentor texts to create images would be helpful for students, and teachers thought that referring to previous lessons on word choice (and the anchor charts they had created then) would be beneficial. They decided to again focus students' attention on word choice as they looked at the winning examples, underlining vivid words that were used when they displayed students' work using the document camera. Linda and Alice put these revisions into practice when they taught the lesson the next day, and students benefitted from seeing the connection between the juicy details in the mentor texts and their peers' word choices for painting mental pictures of their animals.

Our experience with the lesson on vivid details gave teachers confidence in their ability to strengthen lessons through data collection and lesson re*Visioning*. After participating in Lesson Study, Linda said, "I feel so comfortable now. I feel like, 'I could do this!'" Because Lesson Study is organic, holistic, and situated, it utilizes context-specific strengths to meet context-specific challenges.

Information in this chapter describes how Lesson Study can empower you and your colleagues and support your instructional agency as you define and refine best practice for your students. I've described how stepping outside of your comfort zone can help you and your colleagues develop shared knowledge that releases the potential of Lesson Study for continuous improvement.

PERPETUAL MOTION: UNRELENTING IMPROVEMENT OF TEACHING AND LEARNING

Being stationary is not sufficient when it comes to teacher learning. "Teacher preparation" in universities is the beginning of a career-long journey in instructional improvement. As teachers, every year (or every semester), we have new learners to engage with who have differing needs and interests. Every year, there are new resources and ideas to be considered. Every year, we build on our past learning and apply it flexibly to new contexts. We do not stand still, because we are modeling for our students the lifelong learners we hope they will be. Being stagnant is not an option for professional teachers/learners. We are open to change.

Resisting Stagnation

Teaching is one of the few careers where we've had nearly a lifelong apprenticeship before we enter the profession, but that apprenticeship, which Lortie (1975) calls "apprenticeship of observation" (p. 61), may leave us with a repertoire that includes ineffective practices. We also sometimes get stuck in less effective practices that we generate on our own. These might be old favorites that are fun, easy, and enjoyed by both teacher and students but empty of cognitive learning. Engaging, kid-friendly activities may confuse hands-on work with minds-on work, resulting in lessons that "are like cotton candy—pleasant enough in the moment, but lacking long-term substance" (Heineke & McTighe, 2018, p. 10). We may be reluctant to let these favorite activities go, even though they have outlived their usefulness.

Engaging in professional inquiry means recognizing flexibility as a positive process or, as Garcia and O'Donnell-Allen (2015) have labeled it, an opportunity to "wobble" as we push against the status quo. Success does not lie in being "frozen in old practices," but in "a cultural openness to the quest for better ways of doing things" that may represent significant departures from past practice (Danielson, 2015, p. 24).

As we engage in Lesson Study, our "texts" expand beyond books and articles on a required reading list. Our students' responses become texts that we "read," along with professional resources. Reading these texts can keep us moving so that we are alert, not sluggish, and our practices are fluid rather than static. In our quest for better ways of doing things, Lesson Study can help us identify places where we are frozen in old practices and can help us warm to new ones. Lesson Study uncovers new approaches that are informed by the examination of evidence gained through our professional inquiry. Collaboration with colleagues who share similar contexts and concerns makes the insights gained especially helpful. By being the guides to our own professional learning, we resist stagnation and become mobile, active agents of change. With our colleagues, we take a learning stance by asking questions, taking risks, and reflecting on both successes and failures. This is risky business. It means making ourselves vulnerable.

Embracing Uncertainty

Garcia and O'Donnell-Allen (2015) describe dispositions of vulnerable learners as a willingness to pursue questions of consequence, value the perspectives of others, be relentlessly curious, and persist through difficulty.

Learning and change require vulnerability: We become novices when we try something new, but that uncomfortable shakiness can be beneficial, even when it involves falling or failing. Taking a risk, of course, means possible failure. Writing teacher Donald Murray (1996) described the benefits of instructive failure, saying, "I will always fail, and for that I am forever grateful" (p. 49).

Thrill-seekers are accused of playing on the edge of what is safe. The risk is exhilarating, and the results breathtaking. Similarly, we may push the boundaries of what feels safe to us as we try new instructional approaches during the Lesson Study process. We consider new perspectives and ideas as we study, plan, reflect, and revise our lessons and our thinking. We consciously take risks as we try new practices and as we open ourselves to being observed by others while doing so. This learning is risky business and can feel uncomfortable!

When we try something new, we experience a loss of control, a feeling of uncertainty. Remember Allie's response when we first started a Lesson Study on writing with the 5th-grade team at Parker? She was unsure she could do what she had seen in her colleague's classroom and said, "I want to hold my kids' hands and have them do it my way. I have a hard time changing to try it this way" (Collet, 2017, p. 22). But Allie's discomfort with the high level of collaboration changed as she experienced the Lesson Study process. She and her colleagues began to embrace the ambiguity of stepping to the edges of their comfort zone and beyond. This stretch placed them squarely within their own Zones of Proximal Development, that space between what learners can do on their own and what they can do with assistance (Vygotsky, 1978). During Lesson Study, peer collaboration will provide you with the needed assistance. Lesson Study encourages us to constantly take risks to learn something new, as Allie did when she began providing less scaffolding for students.

Some of us naturally avoid risk, never stepping too close to the edge. Others enjoy the excitement of leaping into the unknown. Whether we have a natural aversion to risk or an affinity for adventure, peers can provide assurance as "spotters" ready to assist when we are unsteady. As we ask and then go about answering questions together during the collaborative Lesson Study process, we can revel in the "tension that exists in that space that stands between how you wish things would be and how they are" (Garcia & O'Donnell-Allen, 2015, p. 34).

RISK AND REWARD:
PROFESSIONAL GROWTH THROUGH LESSON STUDY

As director of public relations for John F. Kennedy University, Elizabeth Appell (1979) penned a poem to inspire and motivate learners:

... and then the day came

when the risk to remain

in a bud,

became more painful

than the risk it took to blossom ...

The blossoming we experience in professional growth as teachers is a public unfolding, not a private affair. Even when we try something new behind the closed doors of our classroom, students are our captive audience—not just onlookers, but contributors in the unfolding. Lesson Study pushes even more, because our colleagues are witnesses. But the unfurling enacts ideas that have been co-constructed with them, because we are observing a lesson we have planned together. It is our *ideas* that are under scrutiny, not a solitary product of the observed teacher. So we share in the risk, and we share in the blossoming.

Shared Knowledge

This blossoming includes growth of shared knowledge. Teachers' pedagogical and content knowledge are developed through collegial examination of research and practice. During Lesson Study, we look together at resources, research, and previous lessons. We watch lessons from a student perspective and notice what is working and what needs improving. And we draw on one another's knowledge as we problem-solve and work to understand what has occurred and to revise our thinking. Lewis shares a teacher's reflection on the Lesson Study process: "Having the opportunity to observe students in class, examine their work afterwards and discuss it was also valuable because we typically do not operate like that," she said, "but the knowledge we gained from that process was critical and worthy of our time" (Lewis et al., 2012, p. 372). Lesson Study enables continual growth of knowledge through collaboration.

Interpersonal Resources

Lesson Study also builds interpersonal resources. Skills like active listening, sharing responsibility, demonstrating respect, and nurturing creativity grow through and enhance collaboration. While we plan, observe, and reflect, we interpret information, solve problems together, and manage change. We consider contextual and cultural differences among our teammates and our students as we tune in to contextualization cues—those subtle signaling mechanisms that indicate how we mean what we say—by picking up on both semantic and nonverbal signals (Johnstone, 2008). Careful attention to our own peer interactions and our students' interactions encourages inquiry and enhances communication and instruction. As we engage together in evaluation of practice, the meaning we make is provisional and contextually dependent, sensitive to the diversity of values and culture.

Continuous Improvement

By iteratively following steps in the Lesson Study cycle, teachers reinforce habits and dispositions that support continuous improvement. Mike Rother, author of *Toyota Kata* (2009), a book about process improvement in industry, describes the continuous improvement process in four steps:

1. Develop a shared understanding of the goal and the direction needed toward the goal;
2. Understand the current condition;
3. Establish the next target condition; and
4. Experiment.

The experimenting step in process improvement, according to Rother, is the Plan-Do-Study-Adjust cycle. Lesson Study includes these same elements. Our lesson objectives reflect larger learning goals or standards, and thinking about students' learning progression helps us determine the direction we need to take to move toward the goal. We look at research and currently used resources and plan a lesson that will move our students' learning forward, toward the "next target condition." Then we experiment. One member of our Lesson Study team teaches the lesson while the rest of us gather data. The information we collect includes both process data (how the lesson is developing—what is happening?) and outcome data (the result—are students learning?).

Hopefully, the lesson will not go exactly as planned. If the outcome is exactly what we expected, we have not really learned anything—we have just reinforced what we already knew! As we look closely at differences between expectations and reality, we hone our powers of inference and analysis. We study the data we have collected and reflect together on possible adjustments. Then we re*Vision* our plan for supporting student learning. We revise the lesson, and other teachers on the team (re)teach the lesson to their own students. And the cycle continues.

The Lesson Study process itself is also a focus of continuous improvement. Allie, a teacher on the 5th-grade team at Parker Elementary School, said, "Now that we've done this cycle, I mean, it's just like anything, once you've done it and tried it, it's going to go better the next time." As we hone our skills with this process, it becomes habitual, a natural part of the way we do our work.

Motivation

Lesson Study also increases motivation to improve teaching and learning (Lewis et al., 2012). Watching others do what you want to try, especially if their context is similar to your own, can enhance motivation. Changing the view can also be motivating, which is what happens when we observe a lesson from the students' perspective. The encouragement that members of the Lesson Study team give one another also sustains our drive. Being part of a community of practice increases commitment among teachers (Thoonen, Sleegers, Oort, Peetsma, & Geijsel, 2011).

Agency

Another factor that contributes to motivation during Lesson Study is the emphasis on teacher agency. Teachers are given the responsibility to respond to the specific needs of their students and are empowered as instructional decisionmakers. They have latitude to flexibly use resources and practices rather than following a script or someone else's plan. This agentive role enhances teachers' efficacy—important because teacher efficacy and student achievement are strongly correlated (Moolenaar, Sleegers, & Daly, 2012).

As you re*Vision* your practice through collaborative Lesson Study, you will take risks by trying new approaches and going public with your practice. These risks will reap rewards of increased knowledge, interpersonal resources, habits of continuous improvement, motivation, and agency. Taking risks is, well—risky. But effective teacher learning requires risk-taking and constructive critique (Lieberman & Wood, 2002). Lesson Study's risks will bring benefits for you and your students.

VALUING TEACHING AND TEACHERS

Although an international poll showed that U.S. respondents generally respect and trust teachers (Dolton & Marcenaro-Gutierrez, 2013), legislative attempts to evaluate teachers, high-stakes assessments that label schools, lower-than-average professional salaries, and layers of bureaucratic regulation may leave teachers feeling undervalued (Allegretto, Corcoran, & Mishel, 2004). Another affront to teacher professionalism is the mandated use of scripted curriculum materials that cannot take into account the needs and experiences of learners and teachers. As Garcia and O'Donnell-Allen (2015) emphasize, teachers are professionals, not technicians who must be trained to implement curriculum written by supposed experts outside of the classroom.

In contrast, Lesson Study values teachers by expecting us to be agents of improvement in our own classrooms, instructional decisionmakers responsive to our students' needs, interests, knowledge, and culture. Lesson Study provides for knowledge generation that resists reductionism and systemization (Wieble et al., 2017). Structures for Lesson Study described in this book encourage an expansive view of teacher and student learning. By starting with our own ideas, Lesson Study opens us to critique, learning, and extension of our instructional repertoire (Lieberman & Pointer Mace, 2010). Our continued collaboration builds a culture of participation as we learn with and from our peers and examine and extend our pedagogical knowledge.

Teachers have the opportunity to positively impact not just test scores, but learning and life outcomes of students (Chetty, Friedman, & Rockoff, 2011). By empowering teachers as agents for change, Lesson Study acknowledges the immense value that teachers have for students and their tremendous potential to impact a shared future. By participating in the Lesson Study process, you take an active role in making decisions that affect your own work.

While valuing teaching and teachers, we are also valuing learning and learners. Through Lesson Study, teachers develop "eyes to see children" (Lewis, Perry, & Murata, 2006, p. 7) in ways that acknowledge the funds of knowledge students bring to the classroom (González, Moll, & Amanti, 2006). Students' strategic knowledge and experiences are considered during planning, noted during observation, and incorporated during lesson revision.

CONTEXT MATTERS

I more fully understood how much context matters through my work at Parker Elementary School. The students at this school had made great strides with their learning but were not yet meeting state requirements for achievement on standardized tests. Teachers had a year to turn things around on their own; otherwise, the school would be taken over by outsiders. The pressure in the school was palpable. It was difficult for me to imagine how teachers could do their best teaching and students their best learning with such tension. As the district literacy coordinator, I'd been tasked with supporting the school in improving writing achievement, since data analysis revealed that students' scores on the state writing assessment would make or break their performance requirements. The 5th-grade teaching team was targeted because students' growth on test scores from 4th to 5th grade was an important metric.

Fifth-grade student demographics were similar to those of the school, with 31% of 5th-graders receiving ELL services, 71% receiving free or reduced-cost lunch, and 9% identified for special education services. About the time that I was asked to work with the 5th-grade team, I heard about Lesson Study. I read some articles, bought a book, and was ready to venture forward with what I hoped would make a difference for the hardworking teachers and students at the Parker Elementary School. My hopes were realized, and the school moved from "Turnaround" status to "Performance" status, putting it on solid ground as far as state accountability measures were concerned. The efforts of many contributed to this change, but I am convinced that the Lesson Study work that teachers across the school engaged in played a pivotal role.

Growing with these teachers, and seeing the growth in their students' writing over time, converted me to the Lesson Study process. You'll read more about their story throughout the book. For now, the important changes to note are not only the test scores, but the teachers' changed agency, empowerment, and efficacy. Teachers recognized their own roles as agents for change as they constructed knowledge that contextualized effective teaching practices to meet their students' unique needs. Lesson Study supported this learning. Planning together provided opportunities to study evidence-based practices and determine how they might be used. Observation allowed them to see these practices in action, considering instruction from both teacher and learner perspective. Structures for reflection and analysis supported revision and ongoing improvement. Because Lesson Study is a contextualized form of professional development that values the creation of local knowledge, the plan for change was sensitive to teachers' individual strengths and needs. The instruction they planned was also sensitive to the individual needs of their students.

Lesson Study contributed to increases in teachers' collaboration and sense of efficacy, enhanced their instruction, and supported increases in student achievement. In an era where school reform often restricts teacher agency, Lesson Study provided structures that acknowledged teachers' professionalism, creating home-grown improvement.

In schools where students excel, teachers are highly regarded and trusted, enjoy significant autonomy, and use curriculum flexibly (National Union of Teachers, n.d.). This book makes the case for Lesson Study as a way for teachers to embody these attributes through contextualized professional development. By examining past practice (their own and others') and embracing uncertainty and ambiguity as opportunity, Lesson Study creates a climate for ongoing professional growth and school improvement that values teaching and teachers. Lesson Study empowers teachers and supports their agency as they define and refine best practice for their students.

Reflect and Respond

1. *Read* and annotate the following quote:

   Improving something as complex and culturally embedded as teaching requires the efforts of all the players, including students, parents, and politicians. But teachers must be the primary driving force behind change. They are best positioned to understand the problems that students face and to generate possible solutions.
   —James Stigler and James Hiebert, *The Teaching Gap*, 1999, p.35

   Reflect & Respond: What does this quote mean to you?

2. *Read* one of the following:

   - A Different Approach to Teacher Learning: Lesson Study: http://www.americanradioworks.org/documentaries/teaching-teachers/
   - About Lesson Study: https://lessonresearch.net/about-lesson-study/why-lesson-study/

- Re-Envisioning the One-Room Schoolhouse: https://tinyurl.com/Ch1-Re-Envisioning

Reflect & Respond: What is Lesson Study? Define it in your own words or ·draw a visual describing Lesson Study.

3. ***Read:***

Life as a teacher begins the day that you realize that you are always a learner.
　　　　　　　　　　　　　　　　　　　　　—Robert John Meehan, 2011

Reflect & Respond: Write about the implications of this quote in relation to Lesson Study for you as a teacher.

Self-Assess: Rate yourself on a 1–5 scale: 1 = I know nothing about Lesson Study to 5 = I know what I need to know to get started. If you don't feel ready to get started, you might consider reviewing additional sources from Activity 2, above.

CHAPTER 2

Challenging Norms of Privacy and Isolation

In *Heart-Centered Teaching*, author Nancy Rosenow (2012) reflects:

> Giant sequoia trees seem as if they should be sturdy enough to weather storms alone. In reality, though, even these magnificent specimens need help. An individual Sequoia growing by itself can be blown over in a strong wind. Only by interlocking roots with other trees can a sequoia survive any kind of squall. There's a lesson for all of us there: Sequoias fare best when they support each other and so do we humans. (p. 87)

In the squalls of school life, collaboration helps teachers support one another. School expectations always seem to be in flux, and, importantly, students' needs shift as they learn. As teachers, we feel the push of these winds of change. When we work on and through them with others, these challenges become opportunities for continual professional growth. Lesson Study provides a structure to support this growth.

The processes and protocols in this book focus collaboration on students' assets and needs. I've provided templates and norms to help guide the work, but Lesson Study is an organic process that is activated by the unique problems of practice identified by each Lesson Study team. As teams work together to solve problems of practice, collaboration strengthens both the process and the products. Open communication increases success. Working together enhances capacity, stretches comfort zones, and increases the meaning and value that Lesson Study teams find in their work.

This chapter considers the benefits of collaboration and suggests how to overcome challenges and develop skills that support effective teamwork. Recommendations for scheduling and sustaining the work of Lesson Study are also described so that you can overcome the barriers of privacy and isolation that are prevalent in school settings.

BENEFITS OF COLLABORATION

Collaboration through Lesson Study improves teaching. Varying perspectives strengthen the work. Teachers' resourcefulness and clarity increase, and walls of isolation are broken down. Let's take a look at how Lesson Study can support these benefits.

Varying Perspectives

During Lesson Study, each teacher's unique background knowledge and past experiences enhance the work. When a team gets together, there may be more than 100 years of combined experience in the room! Team members plug one another's gaps and pool a variety of skills as they plan together. As you work with your Lesson Study team, you can take advantage of group members' varying perspectives by asking:

- What do you think?
- How do you see it?
- How has this worked for you in the past?
- What else have you tried?

By leveraging your differences, your team members' unique strengths can complement one another as you plan.

During the observation phase of Lesson Study, different perspectives are again valuable. Teachers working together through Lesson Study have varying points of view, both literally and figuratively. During an observation, teachers can stand in different spots in the room, focus on different students, or consider different aspects of the lesson. Planning ahead of time what each team member will observe helps you notice different things. Even if teachers have the same focus, though, each may see things differently because of individual perspectives.

When teachers reflect together, varied perspectives strengthen the re*Visioning* process. You build on your own strengths as you share. As you think together with your Lesson Study team, your perspective broadens and you open yourself to new ideas.

Increased Resourcefulness

During Lesson Study, collaboration enhances resourcefulness and creativity. Teachers' days are full to the brim, but Lesson Study can provide thoughtful pauses for worthwhile deliberation. These pauses can be generative when team members ask:

- What resources do we have?
- How could we use these resources differently?
- What else could we try?
- What else might be happening here? (looking for possible causes)

When your team comes to meetings with an attitude of inquiry, Lesson Study can create a wellspring of ideas. Together, teachers "can find better ways to answer the learning needs of students" (Lieberman & Wood, 2002, p. 42). Together, you can question practices that have become stale, generate innovation, and create dynamic learning for yourselves and your students.

Reduced Isolation

Although educational mandates and scripted curricula may tempt teachers to close their doors and teach, collaboration can help teachers collectively push boundaries that impede effective instruction. When teachers have a united voice and evidence about what works in our classrooms, we are in a position to advocate for what are truly best practices in our context. The classroom is a data-rich place. Through Lesson Study, we collect evidence of what works and what is not working.

Lesson Study creates a professional culture that spreads good ideas from room to room. This collaborative work can create community and belonging, breaking down the isolation that drives many teachers from the profession. Even though teachers are surrounded by students all day long, we may feel alone. But when we are oriented in communities of practice, we have a place to contribute and grow, and a sense of belonging.

Lesson Study provides for purposeful talk with adults who share common interests. We strengthen unity as we "go public with our practice" (National Writing Project, 2018) through Lesson Study, bouncing ideas off one another, listening respectfully, and celebrating shared victories. We depend on one another and develop trust, seeing the work as both individual and social. During Lesson Study, the work feels collaborative when we use the word *we* more than *I*. Hanging a sign with those two letters, w-e, in the meeting room is a good reminder.

As we work together in Lesson Study, teaching becomes "a public contribution to be shared, used, shaped, and understood by the community" (Lieberman & Pointer Mace, 2010, p. 80). We help one another grow. Our work becomes an illustration of the Quaker proverb, "Thee lift me and I'll lift thee and we'll ascend together."

More Clarity

Learning from and with others brings clarity to our work. During Lesson Study, we can have new conversations about teaching if we closely examine our practice. We analyze and enhance our own knowledge about teaching when we ask:

- What do we already know about this?
- How do we expect students to respond?
- Why did we get these results?

Figure 2.1. Questions to Support Collaboration

During planning, ask:

- What do you think?
- How do you see it?
- How has this worked for you in the past?
- What else have you tried?
- What resources do we have?
- How could we use these resources differently?
- What else could we try?
- What do we already know about this?
- How do we expect students to respond?

During debrief, ask:

- What did you see?
- What are you wondering?
- Why did we get these results?
- What else might be happening here?
- What should we keep?
- What else could we try?
- What do you think?

To self-assess collaboration, ask yourself:

- Did you listen more than you spoke?
- Did you invite others to contribute and really hear their ideas?
- Did you share your own ideas openly?

Words crystalize our thinking. As we verbalize our ideas, our understanding increases. Through our planning and reflecting conversations, we emphasize instructional practices and make them intentional. Our dialogue gives us new ways of thinking about familiar ideas. The ability to conceptualize an idea and apply it in a variety of ways is promoted as we find the right words to describe our impressions and ideas (Vacca & Vacca, 2008). Together, observation and dialogue create a concrete understanding of concepts. Noticing and naming effective practices helps us understand them better and encourages their use. By articulating our notions, we increase clarity.

CHALLENGES TO COLLABORATION

Richard DuFour, an author and educator who advocates for collaborative teaching environments, focuses on bringing teachers together to analyze and improve their classroom practice. DuFour and Marzano (2011) argue,

> In order to establish schools in which inter-dependence and collaboration are the new norm, we must create the structures and cultures that embed collaboration in the routine practice of our schools, ensure that the collaborative efforts focus on the right work, and support educators as they build their capacity to work together rather than alone. (p. 61)

Although collaborative professional learning is recognized as a means for instructional improvement, effective collaboration is a challenging endeavor. Let's consider how teachers can overcome some of the challenges so that Lesson Study achieves its collaborative potential.

Time

The most commonly declared challenge to collaboration is finding the time. This is a longstanding concern. In 1990, Phillip Schlechty said,

> The one commodity teachers and administrators say they do not have enough of, even more than money, is time: time to teach, time to converse, time to think, time to plan, time to talk, even time to go to the restroom or have a cup of coffee. . . . Time is indeed precious in school. (p. 73)

That statement still rings true. However, it is equally true that in our busy daily teaching schedules, teachers will never *find* the time; we must *make* the time for collaboration. Successful schools are distinguished from unsuccessful ones by the degree to which they plan, inform, and analyze collaboratively (Little, 1982; Waldron & McLeskey, 2010).

There is something miraculous about effective collaboration. Have you felt it? Effective collaboration seems to multiply our minutes and expand our time. We feel less busy when we take the time to pause and reflect. There is value added when we work with others toward common goals. Unfortunately, you may have had some unproductive collaborative experiences in the past. These experiences seem to strip us of precious minutes during our working day. The difference, I've found, is in the structures that are put in place to guide collaborative work. As a member of a Lesson Study team, when you focus your planning on a joint problem of practice, observe with an eye toward that problem, and re*Vision* instruction in ways informed by that planning and observation, I think you'll find that your time working together is time well spent. The discussion prompts and templates throughout this book will guide you in this work.

Some of you already have structures in place that will support Lesson Study. Common planning time is needed. If you don't already have time scheduled for working with your colleagues, you can make it with some creativity and persistence. Suggestions later in the chapter that have been successful in other schools can help you make the time for Lesson Study with your team.

Uncertainty

Even if structures are in place for collaboration, emotional baggage can inhibit professional learning. Feelings of self-doubt can hold teachers back from effective collaboration. Sanitized stories of teaching fill our heads with falsely perfect expectations that make us fearful about sharing our concerns, having others observe our teaching, and carefully examining our own practice. These sanitized stories come from fictionalized super-teachers in the media and from the one-sided stories of self-doubt that we tell ourselves.

I will always remember a call I got from my then-22-year-old daughter, Sara, when she was doing a student-teaching internship in 2nd grade. A unique structure at her university allowed some student teachers to be the sole classroom teacher for a yearlong paid internship. Although support structures were in place, I became her de facto mentor. The phone call I'm referring to came one day during recess, when my daughter was sitting in her car, crying.

"I can't go back in there," she sobbed.

My mind raced, calling upon all my past coaching experiences. What could I do in a brief conversation to give her the courage to head back into class before her students did? We talked for a few minutes and concocted a plan: I would come on Friday so she could observe me teaching her class. Having a plan in place gave her the gumption to push through the next couple of days.

When Friday arrived, I taught a reading lesson. The children gathered at my feet on the carpet as we previewed a story and reviewed vocabulary. Then I sent them off to read with partners. I felt it went well and hoped that observing the lesson had been helpful for my daughter.

It was soon recess, and this time Sara had recess duty, so I walked with her to the playground. She gave me a sideways glance and said, "Mom, you won awards for your teaching, right?"

It became immediately obvious that her question was not implying that my teaching was stellar and worthy of such acknowledgment. Instead, she was wondering how such everyday, run-of-the-mill teaching could be considered award-worthy! Children had wiggled and nudged one another. There were some whose eyes weren't on me. It took a couple of minutes for one boy to transition to reading. In other words, it wasn't the perfect lesson she had been expecting of me *and of herself.* Sara had been holding herself, and her students, to an impossibly high standard. Observing my teaching gave her a necessary dose of realism. After that, we were able to talk productively about improvement.

If you are feeling insecure about going public with your practice through Lesson Study, I hope that you, like my daughter Sara, will find that observing others gives you the confidence to learn. When you observe during Lesson Study, you'll find the unexpected as you tune in to student learning. When colleagues observe in your classroom, they'll feel the same thing. Privately, we hold a standard that no one else expects. Going public with our practice can free us of these unrealistic expectations.

Getting real is messy. Changing something in our practice means that we take a risk and feel vulnerable. We try things in front of our students every day, and that can be intimidating, but having our colleagues present for potential missteps ups the ante. Embarrassment, or fear of it, can inhibit our learning (Newkirk, 2017). It's true, absolutely certain, that something will not go as planned. Thank goodness! It's the unexpected that gives us the opportunity to grow.

It might be helpful to recognize that our self-doubt comes from striving to be better. Our perfectionist view of what we want our teaching to be doesn't align with our current view of what it is. Being kind to ourselves, reminding ourselves that our capacity will increase over time, opens us to instructional improvement. Importantly, Lesson Study shifts our attention from the teaching to the learning, taking the spotlight off the teacher and putting it on students. Since increased student learning is our goal, it makes sense to put our focus there. I hope that shift will increase your comfort with the process.

Sharing

Another human frailty that can get in the way of collaboration is selfishness. I like to think that I am collaborative, that I have the "one for all" attitude. But when I recently finished working on a lesson, I admit that I hesitated before posting my PowerPoint, with all its links and detailed notes, to the Google folder I share with my colleagues. I caught myself thinking, "But I worked so hard on this!" I squelched feelings of selfishness and uploaded that PowerPoint, and the whole folder full of related documents, reminding myself that maybe my colleagues could get something from it that would improve learning for our students. Seeing all of the students in all of our classes as a joint responsibility takes away the sting of selfishness.

For collaboration to have a chance, information, resources, and knowledge need to be freely shared. During Lesson Study, teachers start by sharing our own practice—current problems along with what has worked in the past. We put all of our resources out there for consideration. Going public with our practice leads to improvement, to making good things better.

Guarding against feelings of competition also supports openness. The privatization of teaching is exacerbated by competition. Competition makes us perceive situations as hierarchical: There is only so much room at the top, my wins are your losses, and vice versa. In contrast, an abundance mindset (Covey, 2004) tells us that there are always new chances and opportunities. During Lesson Study, we develop an abundance mindset when we share, when we appreciate, and when we celebrate our colleagues' successes as our successes. During a Lesson Study meeting, if you or a colleague starts talking about what you don't have or can't do, change the story. Talk about what is possible. When teams exhibit an abundance attitude, we energize and inspire one another. We trade selfishness for abundance. As you practice Lesson Study, be a river, not a reservoir. Let your ideas flow and feelings of abundance will increase.

Focus

Efforts at collaboration often suffer from lack of focus. This deficiency can leave teachers feeling that time together has not been well spent. We can avoid a dearth of focus by having clear content and processes for collaborative conversations.

In Lesson Study, content focus emerges from data and dialogue about student work. The focus you and your team members choose should be something you'll really have to wrestle with. Lewis and Hurd (2011) suggest that Lesson Study should focus on something that is persistently difficult for students to learn or for teachers to teach. Identifying a topic and then comparing the real to the ideal can help you identify where to center your efforts for a Lesson Study cycle. The focus should be something members of the group really care about, something that will make a difference in student learning. Details for selecting the content for Lesson Study are included in Chapter 4.

In addition to having a clear content focus, you will want to keep your process efficient to honor participants' time. This book is full of suggestions about process such as guiding questions (like those in Figure 2.1) and pre- and postobservation templates. Use these resources as seems fitting for your group. The important thing is to stay focused on what you want to accomplish and to understand how the Lesson Study cycle will get you there. Buy-in for the process will increase as you see outcomes from Lesson Study.

In my Lesson Study work at Parker Elementary School, teachers were under duress because of their "Turnaround" school status, which had been determined by low test scores. Coming in as an outsider, I felt that presenting protocols to be strictly adhered to would not be well received Instead, I kept myself, as facilitator, very grounded in the protocols, but I posed questions to guide us authentically through the prescribed Lesson Study process. Protocols were a covert guide for me instead of an overt tool for our meetings. Later, after the group was comfortable working together, templates became an efficient tool to guide our work. You or your team can determine (and be flexible about) the role that protocols and templates will play in your work.

A content focus that is urgent and real shakes us out of autopilot, making our collaborative work meaningful. The Lesson Study cycle provides a purposeful structure for accomplishing the work. Having focus in both content and process provides clarity as teachers scrutinize and struggle through a problem together.

SHARED EXPECTATIONS

Effective Lesson Study groups have shared expectations for collaboration. These expectations guide how the work will be done and how teachers will interact with one another during the process. These ideas live in our minds and tell us what we are supposed to (and not supposed to) do. They play a big part in how each member of a group feels, thinks, and acts, including how we respond to one another. They provide order and predictability, helping group members feel safe.

Sociologists call such expectations *norms*, a term that for me invokes negative connotations of restrictive rules. Often, professional development providers will review norms before beginning a session. In many settings, that's expected protocol (there's a norm about norms!). I shy away from this review of rules because it usually feels pejorative to me. As a professional, I don't feel I need to be told to "take care of my own needs" (i.e., go to the bathroom), "listen when others are talking" (I've been saying that to students for years—I think I've got it!), or "be open-minded" (no one thinks they are anything but). For me, these things should go without saying in a professional setting, so when they are stated, it feels deprofessionalizing. When facilitating Lesson Study, I seldom review norms. But that doesn't mean there aren't any.

Developing Underlying Assumptions, Structures, and Skills

Effective Lesson Study is guided by norms that make the work productive, safe, and inclusive. These norms are woven through the protocols and descriptions in this book. As you read, you'll become aware of the ways to do Lesson Study to cultivate this culture. It's about who we are as people, how we treat one another, and how we treat one another's ideas. We can all get better at these things, and as we do, our generous interactions will make collaboration stronger.

Unspoken expectations for interaction develop when people feel part of a group. When group identity is important to us, when we want to belong, we generally adhere to group expectations. These expectations usually develop informally through a shared purpose. Talking explicitly about the process of Lesson Study helps establish underlying expectations.

Focus on Practice. An underlying assumption for Lesson Study is that we can separate the teaching from the teacher. Differences are not simply a matter of style; professionals have a common body of knowledge and practices, and you are working to increase and improve these during Lesson Study. This assumption encourages the team to look deeper than style and personality to analyze how teaching practice works and how it can be enhanced. As teachers understand effective instructional practices, they recognize the space for unique and personalized application along with the aspects that should be firmly in place. This process is embedded in the structures for Lesson Study.

Clarify Process. Having a process to follow during collaboration keeps your team moving toward your objectives. Phases of the Lesson Study cycle (study, plan, observe, reflect, re*Vision*, reteach) guide you toward your goal of improved instruction and keep the conversation focused on learning. All team members need clarity about what Lesson Study is and what it is not. Reading this book together will give you that shared understanding.

Maintain Focus. Inquiry is the essential element of Lesson Study, so the clear focus you identify for a Lesson Study cycle should propel your desire to investigate, to analyze and study together. Pursuing the questions your group has identified provides challenge and authentic purpose, which increase motivation and engagement (Senn, 2012; Shuck, Reio, & Rocco, 2011). Because you have identified the problem for yourselves, you see how the process can be of value. Maintaining focus keeps the work moving forward.

Define Roles. Lesson Study includes both collaboratively social and individually agentive aspects. Each team member is actively engaged when openly sharing, planning, and reflecting. There is work for everyone. In addition to shared responsibilities, it can be helpful to define roles. These roles might be stable and capitalize on individual strengths, or rotate among group members. A facilitator ensures protocols are followed. Data and research are brought forward. Careful notes also need to be taken. After a planning session, someone needs to polish up the lesson plan before the lesson is taught. Whether roles are fluid or stable, ensuring that these responsibilities are covered is important to the Lesson Study process.

Communicate. Communication is a two-way process, and all can work to improve it. After meeting with your Lesson Study team, you might conduct a self-evaluation of your own communication skills:

- Did you listen more than you spoke?
- Did you invite others to contribute and really hear their ideas?
- Did you share your own ideas openly?

There is a balance to group communication that improves with attention.

It's also important for Lesson Study teams to decide how they will communicate between meetings. Quick conversations in the hall may leave someone out of the loop; group emails or texts ensure everyone has the same information and expectations. Online tools allow for asynchronous communication that works within everyone's schedule.

Be Open. As described above, effective communication includes genuinely listening to others' ideas. For Lesson Study to be effective, teachers need to listen with a willingness to change. Being open to new ideas isn't easy and can create tension—both internal and within the group. Remember the response of the Parker 5th-grade teachers described in the Introduction? When they were working on providing less scaffolding during writing instruction, Allie said, "I want to hold my kids' hands and have them do it my way." Linda said, "I'd have a hard time changing to try it this way." Allie and Linda were beginning to see wisdom in not overscaffolding, but they acknowledged how difficult it was to make this shift. Their willingness to say this out loud was an indication that they were actually going to give it a try.

Be Kind. Above all, be kind. Aspire to give credit to others for their contributions. Publicly praise. Forgive other group members' mistakes, because you will make them, too. Work to keep a positive attitude, bring a sense of humor, and be respectful. Gracefully acknowledge when you fall short and graciously support others when they do. I have seen many Lesson Study groups work together in this way, and it can be true for your group, too.

Fostering Effective Expectations

The more individuals see group membership as beneficial, the more likely they will be to abide by group norms, so job number one for fostering effective expectations is to keep the work purposeful and productive. This goes a long way toward keeping team members focused and kind. However, that doesn't mean there won't be times when you step out of the box of positive group expectations. There will be times when it is more than you can do to be upbeat, when you don't have the energy to do unto others as you would have them do unto you. The same will be true for other members of your team. That is part of the beauty of group-work. Team members can be there to lift one another when these moments come.

And there are times when our lives seem made up of these moments. The beginnings of my work with Parker seemed this way. Because of the pressure they were under as a Turnaround school, teachers were living on the edge of their emotional reserves. They were still putting their best foot forward for the kids, but adult interactions sometimes broke down. Even with this group (perhaps especially there), I wasn't explicit about stating norms. There was occasional venting, but the conversation usually came around quickly once we focused on the work to be done. There were so many frustrations on the surface, but deep down, we all cared about the kids.

As I think back on that time, I realize I did some things to keep Lesson Study at Parker a positive place. Sometimes I actively drew our attention back to the work at hand: A glance at the clock and a comment ("Oh, wow, we've only got 15 minutes left!") helped us refocus. When negative explanations were expressed, I tried to offer an alternative explanation ("I wonder if . . ."). When someone wasn't participating, I tried to draw the teacher in. You have done this, too, in other settings, and when you are alert to such situations during your group interactions, you are doing your part to make Lesson Study successful for your group.

If negatives norms are developing, these attempts might not be enough. A direct conversation might still be helpful or even necessary. Keep in mind, though, that while compliance can be enforced, emotions can't be. So thinking through the whys of negative responses is essential.

SUPPORTING, SCHEDULING, AND SUSTAINING THE WORK

Getting the Lesson Study process rolling requires initiative and planning. Your group needs time and expectations for this shared work. The following sections give suggestions for getting started and options for creating space in your schedule for the process.

Initiating Lesson Study

Providing an optimal learning environment for kids requires more than individual planning. Group effort will more likely produce a school with processes and practices that operate "in the best interest of students" (Gallagher, 2015, p. 2). We live "in a world that is ever in flux," offering the opportunity for continual professional growth (Garcia & O'Donnell-Allen, 2015, p. 131). Lesson Study is a cycle of continuous improvement that supports such lifelong learning.

You have a role in this continuous improvement process. If Lesson Study is new to your team, you are in a position to launch and support the work. This might include sharing with team members what you know about Lesson Study or supporting group efforts as you learn together about the process.

My colleague Savanna Gragg developed an outline for an introductory meeting about Lesson Study that we've used to get the process started (see Appendix A). In this meeting, we begin by posting sticky notes on a K-W-L (Know, Want-to-Know, Learn) chart, sharing what we know or want to know about Lesson Study. We read and discuss a quote about teachers' role in improving instruction, and then we read a short article about Lesson Study. We draft our own definition of Lesson Study, create a graphic that captures what is important to us, and then finally revisit our K-W-L chart and add new ideas. We've found that this introduction provides basic information about Lesson Study and establishes the collaborative approach we'll take throughout the work. It also creates a tone of genuine inquiry where conversations stem from curiosity and questions are posed in the spirit of exploration.

Whether your group has an appointed facilitator or that is a rotating role, the facilitator's job is to keep the work moving forward, not to foist ideas upon others. Group structure should be devoid of hierarchy. It's important that everyone feels that there is a level playing field, that everyone's ideas are welcome. When I train Lesson Study facilitators, I ask them to think about their position—both figuratively and literally. If they stand in front of the group (for example, to use a PowerPoint on a screen), it sends a different message than if everyone is seated together around a table. Considering these nuances helps build the collaborative culture that we're all in this together. A facilitator guides the process but does not determine the destination.

Scheduling the Work

Because time is a fixed commodity, you may need to think strategically and creatively about scheduling for Lesson Study. Lesson Study works best when teachers who teach the same course or grade level are available to meet at the same time. However, even teachers of different subjects can use Lesson Study to improve instruction. The group unites around their common teaching goals.

You may already have common planning time with a group of colleagues interested in "working on the work" (Schlechty, 2002). In that case, study, planning, reflecting, and re*Visioning* can occur during that time. Only the observation portion of the Lesson Study cycle will require adjustments. If common planning time isn't currently available, you can consider the ideas below to make time for Lesson Study. Perhaps restructuring schedules, altering staff utilization, or adding or buying time can open opportunities for Lesson Study.

Restructuring. Organizing available time differently can open windows for Lesson Study. One school took the professional development days allocated on the district calendar and divided them up into chunks. Instead of having one day a quarter for PD, teachers stayed after school eight times for an extra hour. Then, when the PD day rolled around, they took the day with their families, since those hours had already been logged. Their principal felt confident that the time had been better spent by teachers' regular involvement with Lesson Study than by a full day of PD that was less aligned with teachers' day-to-day practices.

Through careful scheduling, time for common planning can be created within the school day. Teachers already have guaranteed planning time, so students' specials or electives can be scheduled to ensure that teachers with common interests are planning at the same time. Some of this time can then be dedicated to Lesson Study. Creating such a schedule is like putting together a complex jigsaw puzzle; principals usually welcome teachers' ideas for rescheduling when they come with a specific plan in mind.

Many schools and districts have altered students' schedules to create time for common planning. Late-start or early-release days open time for collaboration within the teachers' workday, but they require clear communication with the community about the rationale for such a strategy.

Altering Staff Utilization. Thinking flexibly about how students are grouped and who is serving them can open time for Lesson Study. For example, when 4th-grade book buddies visit their 1st-grade friends once a month, the 4th-grade team conducts an observation. Peer tutoring is an effective intervention for all students, benefitting both academic and affective aspects of learning (Bowman-Perrott et al., 2013; Miller, Topping, & Thurston, 2010), so this adjustment is a win for students, too.

Another school has utilized school staff, parent volunteers, and community partners to involve students in monthly community service projects while their teachers collaborate and observe. Service learning benefits students' attitudes toward self and school and increases their social skills and academic performance (Celio, Durlak, & Dymnicki, 2011).

Some STEAM schools, working to increase students' opportunities in the arts, have had special-subject teachers plan block experiences that engage students in integrated opportunities for music, visual art, and movement. While students experience these extended enrichment opportunities, teaching teams work together.

In another school, administrators have stepped in to open opportunities for collaboration. Rotating through different grade levels, an administrator conducted a monthly "pep assembly" where students' efforts (both academic and social) were celebrated. This assistant principal said the assemblies helped build a positive school culture, and they provided time for teachers of the same content to collaborate.

Conscientious teachers are reluctant to be out of their classrooms unless they know something valuable is going on for their students in their absence. Activities that involve peer tutoring, service learning, arts integration, and recognition of students' efforts can create meaningful experiences for students while their classroom teachers are engaged in meaningful learning of their own.

Adding and Buying Time. If restructuring or shifting responsibilities doesn't seem like a viable option for your team, you could consider buying time through substitute teachers or adding time to the workday for collaboration. Schools may have discretionary funds available to hire substitute teachers. With careful planning, you can stretch these funds a long way. For example, in my Lesson Study work at some schools, we have used just two subs, who rotated through all grade levels throughout the day, to provide time for observations. We've been able to schedule these observation times adjacent to a planning period, allowing for reflection and re*Vision* immediately afterward.

Although I'd consider adding time to the school day as a last resort because teachers' days are already full, time for collaborative Lesson Study can increase efficiency and reduce the amount of individual out-of-school time teachers spend preparing. Still, if you plan to come to school before contract hours or stay late, it would be nice to have salary compensation. Most U.S. schools or districts have federal Title II, Part A funds available that are specifically designated for teachers' professional learning. Targeting these funds to pay teachers for work beyond contracted hours is an option to consider. Some schools, like Parker Elementary, will have school improvement funds available that can be appropriately targeted for this work.

Purposefully combining classes or grouping students together for constructive purposes creates a win-win situation for students and teachers. If you don't already have collaborative time built into your work schedule, you might consider how alternative staff utilization, restructuring schedules, and adding or buying time could free you up for the impactful work of Lesson Study.

OVERCOMING PRIVACY AND ISOLATION

Like the giant sequoias that stand together for strength, collaboration strengthens teachers and teaching. The time necessary for collaboration is not auxiliary. Instructional improvement is not an "extra duty." Collaborative work to strengthen teaching and learning should be at the core of teachers' work week. It is essential for school success. At a school where such work had become routine, the principal said, "Teachers can no longer just teach behind their doors and then at the end of the year send their kids on to the next grade level." She created opportunities for "complete deprivatization of practice." These words may sound harsh, but one teacher said, "It's kind of funny because a lot of people in our district call us Disneyland because you walk in and it's a happy place." Having everyone pulling in the same direction reduces stress and increases satisfaction.

The structures of Lesson Study support effective collaboration. Lesson Study situates teachers as knowledgeable collaborators for critical evaluation of their own practice and for pedagogical problemsolving. Teaching is joint and public, an approach that contributes to continuous improvement (Rust, 2009). Working together, teachers are more competent, able, and experienced than any one of us would be alone.

Studies highlight the importance of offering opportunities for collaboration, reflection, and inquiry so teachers can work together to improve learning (Bean & Lillenstein, 2012). As the teachers at Parker Elementary School began to embrace the shared practices of Lesson Study, Kim said, "There are things in the lesson plan I never would have thought of because I'm brainstorming with others. It's that collaborating." Making teaching a shared and public practice supports improved instruction.

Reflect and Respond
---

1. *Review* these ideas for creating a teacher-powered school.

   • https://www.teacherpowered.org/guide

   Reflect & Respond: Have you had collaborative experiences where groups stormed? If so, did you move past this stage? How? If not, why not?

2. *Watch* this video:

   • https://tinyurl.com/mills-collaborative-inquiry

   Reflect & Respond: At the beginning of this video, Ms. Wilson poses several questions about collaboration. Write down one of them and respond.

3. *Read:* "I can do things you cannot; you can do things I cannot; together we can do great things."

   —attributed to Mother Teresa, in Park, 2015, p. 105

   Reflect & Respond: What are the strengths you bring to your Lesson Study team? List a few. Next, write down a couple of strengths for each person on your team. You might want to get together with your Lesson Study group and compare your lists. Discuss how team members' strengths complement one another.

   Self-Assess: Respond to the three self-assessment questions in Figure 2.1. How are you doing?

CHAPTER 3

Lesson Study as Contextualized Learning

Miranda Escamilla shepherded her kindergartners into the classroom and to their spots on the rug. They had just experienced their first fire drill, and they were excited to talk about it.

"I'm so proud of you," Ms. Escamilla applauded. "You did a great job with the fire drill. Let's think about what you did. What did you do first?"

"We be-ed quiet!" one little boy, an English learner, piped in.

"Yes, you were quiet," Ms. Escamilla responded. "And what did you do first while you were being quiet?"

"We lined up!"

"Yes, first you lined up, and then what did you do next?"

"We walked down the hall."

"And then what?"

"We went outside."

"So first you lined up, then you walked down the hall, then you went outside. What happened after that?"

"We waited for the bell."

"Then what?"

"We came back!"

"So let's see if I got this right. First, we lined up, then walked down the hall, then we went outside and waited for the bell, then we came back in. Is that right?"

"YES!"

"When we think about the order that things happened in, that's called sequencing," Ms. Escamilla explained. "Can you say that with me? It's kind of hard for Ms. Escamilla to say. Let's say it together."

"Sequencing!"

"What was that again?"

"Sequencing!"

"So, we're going to be learning about sequencing today, because it's important to know how to remember things in order. Today we're going to try it with a book called *The True Story of the Three Little Pigs.*"

Down the hall, in a 4th-grade room, Bailey Chenier launched a math lesson on rounding by asking, "Why might you use rounding?"

One student explained, "Say you have thirty-six kids at a party, but you're not sure if there's actually thirty-six, you might round it to the nearest ten."

The next student suggested you might round if someone asked you what time it is. Another said you might round "if you don't know how long you're going to be gone for something." Building on these real-life examples, students launched into the lesson with increased interest in rounding, the topic of that day's math lesson.

What do these two lessons have in common? They are both grounded in the context and interests of students. Students' lives are full of experiences offering rich connections to the curriculum. When teachers draw on this knowledge and build conceptual bridges between home and school, engagement increases as students see the relevance of the work. Miranda captured students' excitement as first-time fire-drillers. Bailey asked a simple question that opened the door for students to contextualize their learning, giving them the space to make personal connections to the content. These teachers had acquired the habit of considering context, culture, and students' interests and needs, building on funds of knowledge that students brought to their school-learning experience (Moll, Amanti, Neff, & González, 2006).

In this chapter, we'll consider why context matters and I'll introduce you to some of the schools where I've participated in Lesson Study—schools that we'll visit throughout the book as rich examples of collaborative work and contextualized student learning.

WHY CONTEXT MATTERS

Re*Visioning* through Lesson Study provides the opportunity to problem-solve around the unique students sitting in your classroom, planning learning experiences that reflect and respect their diversity. Lesson Study supports instruction that is sensitive to context. As you work with colleagues in Lesson Study, you can re*Vision* learning to strengthen connections to context, both the context within and the context outside of the classroom. As you teach, you are likely already making connections between academic abstractions and students' lived realities. Lesson Study gives you space to think through and increase such connections.

During collaborative planning, you think with colleagues about context, culture, and students' interests and needs. You ask yourself, "What experiences have students had with this concept?" "How could we help students make connections to their own background knowledge?" Then you make plans to incorporate relevant experiences strategically into instruction.

Before an observation, team members anticipate how students might respond based on their previous experiences. For example, during a Lesson Study on close reading, teachers felt the discussion of "aha" moments as aids to understanding themes would be supported by students' connections to a popular movie they had seen. Including students' at-home experiences as resources reduces the insularity of classroom performance (Moll et al., 2006). As you notice connections students make on their own, you can use these experiences strategically as anchors to new learning, bringing students' experiences to the center.

No two classes are the same. No two children are the same. Because learning will reflect these differences, teaching must reflect it, too. During Lesson Study observations, your awareness of the unique attributes of each class and each student will increase because you are freed from teaching to focus on learning. Noticing these differences will draw your attention to variation within your own classes and will spur ideas for how to respond to such variation. When one of Bailey's colleagues observed the math lesson described at the beginning of this chapter, she knew her "chatty class" wouldn't respond in the same way. She added a chance for partner talk early in the lesson to give the English language learners in her classroom an opportunity to process. This instructional adjustment was sensitive to students' individual needs.

Although Lesson Study was created in the fairly homogeneous Japanese culture, it is a valuable vehicle for supporting responsive instruction. When team members ask themselves about context and culture throughout the planning, observing, and reflection phases of Lesson Study, we gain a better understanding of how instruction can be strengthened through connections with students' previous experiences, and we build the habit of incorporating such connections. We develop a clearer understanding of how to plan instruction that is sensitive to context, that reflects and respects the varied cultures found in our classrooms.

The human capacity for learning makes possible an almost infinite variety of responses, so effective teaching must be responsive to people, place, and culture. Lesson Study captures the diversity of human learning and helps us design and refine lessons for the unique students in our classrooms.

LESSON STUDY IN VARYING CONTEXTS

A hallmark of effective instruction is flexibility and responsiveness, not rigidity and repetition (Danielson, 2011). The goal of Re*Visioning* through Lesson Study is not to create homogenized lessons. Rather, the goal is to uncover why and how aspects of instruction work within specific contexts. Participating in Lesson Study can enhance understanding of effective pedagogy and help team members refine instruction in contextually specific ways.

Throughout this book, you'll read about Lesson Study with teachers from a variety of contexts. I hope that sharing these examples will help you see yourself in the Lesson Study process. Let's get to know these contexts and the teachers and students who teach and learn there.

Lesson Study in a Rural School

Changing demographics and political tensions in the United States have highlighted the need to consider context and have increased attention to rurality. Rural schools often have a revolving door of less experienced teachers due to remote locations, fewer resources, and lower pay.

I talked about these issues with Jean Hill, who began her teaching career at a rural school, where she experienced challenges because of isolation. She felt a need for "purposeful, meaningful, and strategic support through collaboration with educators within [her] school," but she didn't have that opportunity. In her small rural school, Jean didn't have the chance to say, "I don't understand," or to ask, "How might this work in my classroom, with my students?" She felt that a lack of resources limited her ability to help herself and her students. "Teachers must be able to purposefully and organically collaborate with each other in order to sustain the future of rural education in the United States," she said. Lesson Study provides the framework for such collaboration.

Rural teachers may also experience a mismatch between purchased materials and the experiences of their students. In rural districts, leaders sometimes feel it is unrealistic to expect ever-changing teachers to create their own curriculum, so they purchase resources to support instruction. To be effective, however, these resources must be used flexibly, in ways that fit students' backgrounds and needs. Lesson Study can be a way to provide for authentic collaboration and use impersonal curriculum materials to grow lessons that are personalized for students and that highlight effective practices for teachers. The experiences of rural teachers demonstrate the role Lesson Study can play in instructional improvement.

Throughout this book, we'll peek in on Lesson Study in the rural community of Berryville, Arkansas. According to the 2010 census, the population of this community was 5,356, but Berryville schools draw from the hills and fields of the surrounding area. The community is mostly White, with a growing Latinx population (25%). This changing social structure reflects the situation in many small towns and cities in the South and Midwest, as schools and communities experience cultural shifts.

Berryville's median family income (for 2008–2012) was about $38,000. Berryville is the home of gun manufacturing companies as well as the International Defensive Pistol Association. Many residents in the county work in production; farming, fishing, and forestry are also strong industries.

Berryville School District has four schools: an elementary (pre-K–2), an intermediate school (grades 3–5), a middle school (grades 6–8), and a high school (grades 9–12). The Berryville community comes together to support Berryville Bobcat athletes, with Friday night home football games being a favorite fall event.

During the 2017–2018 school year, Berryville schools began using Lesson Study in their work with instructional coaching and professional learning communities. Christy Graham, the district's school improvement specialist, said the changes Lesson Study brought to their district were transformative. "Teachers are now seeing their professional development as valuable and purposeful," she said. "Lesson Study has enabled our schools' educators to collaborate and learn from each other's strengths. . . . Our teachers see the time spent on Lesson Study as necessary to better target and improve their instructional challenges." Throughout the book, we'll see how these teachers learned together through Lesson Study.

Lesson Study in Schools with Underserved Populations

Although there is broad diversity of student populations in the United States, this diversity is underrepresented in teacher demographics. The National Center for Educational Statistics (U.S. Department of Education, 2016) reports that 51% of K–12 students were nonwhite in the 2015–2016 school year, but only 20% of public education teachers were racial or ethnic minorities. This discrepancy suggests that students may not be educated in ways that are reflective of and responsive to their cultural identities. By emphasizing context during planning and by focusing attention on how students respond to instruction, Lesson Study can improve this condition and better prepare all students for meaningful participation in our diverse society.

All students possess a rich set of cultural practices and knowledge that can be foundational for learning (Gay, 2010). For students of color, these robust experiences may not align with norms of public schools. Teachers and administrators bring their own norms to school and may be unaware of connections between curriculum and students' experiences that could build understanding. Similarly, teachers may be unaware of cultural expectations that differ from their own and may misinterpret students' actions. For example, students who do not speak up in class may be viewed as less interested, although for some this is the expression of cultural background.

If you are a teacher of children from varied cultures, you may want to build upon cultural connections and be sensitive to students' cultural norms. It can be hard, however, to see enough and do enough. Inviting colleagues into your classroom to observe your students and then discussing with them what they see brings insights about connections between culture and classroom context. This happened for us during Lesson Study at Stilwell High School in Oklahoma.

Stilwell High School is adjacent to the town's middle and elementary schools. In Stilwell, the median family income is about $25,000. The high school has about 650 students, with 70% being Native American, predominantly from the Cherokee tribe.

In the United States, Native Americans are a traditionally marginalized and underserved group. As early as 1879, Native American day schools and boarding schools provided education and resources but restricted freedom and were a means of cultural assimilation (Holm, 2005). Students' own cultures were squelched as children who attended these schools were given European American names and haircuts and forbidden to speak their own languages. Julie Davis (2001) argues that harsh conditions in these schools "fueled the drive for political and cultural self-determination" among Native Americans (p. 20), with tribal nations subsequently calling for community-based schools. Stilwell High School might be considered one such school, since the school population is determined by geographic, rather than racial, boundaries.

Lesson Study work at Stilwell began with three teachers and an outside facilitator, Angelia Greiner. Angelia is a doctoral student at my university and, as she says, "a card-carrying Cherokee," although she was raised in mainstream White culture and only later developed an intense interest in her cultural heritage. Angie is a high school English teacher with a focus on culturally sustaining pedagogy. One of the three English teachers Angie worked with at Stilwell High also has Native American roots. Lisa Sawney is one-quarter Cherokee, although she says she was "raised White." However, her husband, Joey, was raised in a very traditional Cherokee home, and as she considers the needs of her traditionally raised Native students, she often asks herself, "What would Joey do?" Tasha Workman, who teaches English and World Literature, identifies as multiracial and has been at Stilwell High for 7 years. The third teacher, Charity West, is White and has taught in Stilwell schools for over 20 years, often serving in leadership roles.

All three teachers grew up within 150 miles of the school. Although all of the teachers have knowledge of their students' backgrounds, their instructional approaches were guided more by standards and assessments than by their students' cultural repertoires. Nevertheless, knowledge of their students' backgrounds always informed their instruction, and Lesson Study brought this knowledge to the fore. The teachers had previously had extensive training on Professional Learning Communities, and they said that Lesson Study was the missing piece to make their collaborative work meaningful and impactful. Working in a school where students' rich cultural heritage was so different from my own was also a wonderful learning opportunity for me.

Throughout the book, you'll also hear about Lesson Study in other schools with other underserved populations, such as Old Wire Elementary School (described below). We'll also return frequently to examples of Lesson Study at Parker Elementary, the Turnaround school highlighted in the Introduction, which has a high population of Latinx students, many of them English language learners.

Lesson Study in a Sanctioned School

Currently, the paradigm guiding educational reform focuses on using external assessments to measure school success and imposing mandates and sanctions rather than building capacity. Reform efforts guided by such assumptions have unintended consequences.

Accountability systems tied to school reform may create an overemphasis on testing, constrain the curriculum, decrease teacher efficacy, and reduce teachers' responsiveness to specific needs of the student populations. Policies may include top-down decisionmaking that reduces teachers' flexibility and their use of local knowledge. When teachers' decisionmaking power is constrained, their lower self-efficacy impacts how well students learn (Bruce, Esmonde, Ross, Dookie, & Beattie, 2010; Valli & Buese, 2007).

In high-achieving schools, teachers feel little impact from accountability policies. Students' high test scores relieve them of reformers' scrutiny. However, high-poverty schools disproportionately feel the pressures of such reforms.

Earlier in this book, I have described the pressure teachers at Parker Elementary School experienced when their school was classified as a Turnaround school. State and federal policies created a high-stakes environment that left teachers feeling overwhelmed, frustrated, and angry. However, using Lesson Study, teachers' professionalism was acknowledged and accessed. Rather than answering to imposed accountability systems, teachers answered to one another as they worked together to improve instruction. We'll revisit Parker throughout the book, illustrating how Lesson Study supported instructional changes that targeted the needs of their unique students and helped them move to classification as a Performance school.

Lesson Study with Preservice Teachers

Another group with whom I've experienced Lesson Study is preservice teachers. I feel lucky that part of my job is to spend time at Old Wire Elementary School in Rogers, Arkansas, and work with teachers and student-teaching interns there. When I walk into Old Wire, the students bring an immediate smile to my face. They are full of energy and optimism. They flood through the doors at 7:10 every morning, excited to be together and learn. My student teachers are equally excited to learn there. They are glad to have the chance to put their book learning into practice with students in a high-poverty school, knowing that working with this population will help them hone their teaching skills.

At Old Wire, about 90% of students qualify for free or reduced-price lunch; about 64% are Hispanic and 27% White, with small percentages of Black, Native American, and Pacific Islanders. About a third of students are classified as having limited English proficiency, although a much larger percentage speaks English as a nonnative language.

Student teachers in my program are called interns. They have completed an undergraduate degree in education but haven't yet earned a teaching license. The master of arts in teaching program and yearlong student-teaching experience prepare them to receive their teaching credentials.

In our program, interns are usually at their internship schools 4 days a week and attend courses on campus on the fifth day. They experience placements in three different classrooms, working with students in a range of grades. During each placement, interns gradually assume full-time teaching responsibilities. Interns are supported by their mentors (cooperating teachers) and by me (their university liaison). Lesson Study is one of the ways I offer support to interns.

Student teaching is the final test for those who want to teach. Interns have the chance to demonstrate their ability to plan and deliver effective instruction. Caires and Almeida (2007) describe the student-teaching experience as "the opportunity to stand face to face with the challenges and demands of the teaching profession" (p. 516). Just like licensed teachers, student teachers have different challenges based on their own strengths and weaknesses. Student teachers may be hesitant to discuss concerns with their mentor teachers because they want to maintain the impression of competence. Lesson Study gives interns a safe forum to discuss specific challenges with one another. Because a lesson is jointly planned, everyone feels ownership for the lesson's success, and no one is singled out as lacking. In the process of re*Visioning*, interns learn effective practices that are diffused beyond the single lesson they've experienced together.

SUPPORTING A POSITIVE CULTURE FOR TEACHING

Teachers may feel manacled by requirements when educational reform efforts call for rigid, formulaic teaching. Yet you and I know that all students are not the same, and they don't all learn in the same ways! Unique students and diverse student populations call for attention to culture and context. Students vary enormously in their talents, interests, and backgrounds. Skilled teachers build on these strengths, using what students already know to support further learning.

As a participant in Lesson Study, you become more accurate in predicting how your students will respond, and this helps you design potentially effective lessons. But there's more. As learning unfolds, you pay close attention to how things are going and you act, and react, accordingly. Extra eyes on students during Lesson Study observations support this process. The more you and your teammates discuss students' responses to instruction, the more aware of them you are as they transpire. As you contextualize teaching practices to meet your students' unique needs, you become agents for effective change. By valuing students' culture—their values, beliefs, and attitudes—you are also supporting a teaching culture that has positive values about your own role as a professional.

In all of the places I've described above, teachers have collected data about their students' learning so that they can flexibly meet the needs of their students. They are teaching in ways that their experiences with their own students prescribe, rather than ways that are prescribed by off-the-shelf manuals. Through Lesson Study, these teachers have used their professional voices to talk about their teaching and to align their teaching with the needs of their students. They have demonstrated why context matters.

Reflect and Respond
---

1. *Read* and annotate the following quote:

> Schools are nested within their external environment, which includes parents, the community in which they are situated, the economic conditions present in those communities and the values espoused by that community; curriculum standards, achievement expectations, programmatic requirements, and other policy directives; and other social agencies that serve children. The external environment can contribute to successful student outcomes and build resilience among students.
>
> —Bascia, 2014, p. 10

Reflect & Respond: Choose one of the elements of context described in the above quote and write about its impact in the context where you teach or a school you are familiar with.

2. *Read or watch* one of the following:

- https://tinyurl.com/Ch3-Turnaround
- https://www.weareteachers.com/rural-teacher/
- https://tinyurl.com/Ch3-Diverse-Texts

Reflect & Respond:

- What teacher attributes support success in the context you considered in the above article or video?

3. *Read* the following quote:

> Teachers can positively affect the learning outcomes of all students in all contexts.
>
> —Fenwick & Cooper, 2013, p. 108

Reflect & Respond: How can teachers develop this core belief?

Self-Assess: How comfortable are you teaching students whose culture differs from your own? Rate yourself on a 1–4 scale, 1 = I am very uncomfortable to 4 = I am very comfortable teaching students whose culture differs from my own. Do you need to improve this comfort level? If so, how will you do that? If you are already very comfortable teaching students whose culture differs from your own, what helped you develop this attitude?

PART II

LAYERS OF THE LESSON STUDY PROCESS

CHAPTER 4

Purposeful Planning
Teachers as Designers

In recent decades, teachers have felt increasingly disempowered and professionally marginalized (Priestley, Edwards, Priestley & Miller, 2012). This is an international trend that, fortunately, may not be felt on an individual level, because the culture of teaching varies by school. Teachers' professional voices are stronger in some schools than in others, and Lesson Study is an opportunity to strengthen that professional voice.

If you are working at a school where purchased curricula are imposed, you may wonder, as I did when working in a school with such expectations, how to exercise your professional voice. But I learned that even within contexts where instruction is prescribed, the ways in which that prescribed instruction is enacted provide space for design and agency. There is room for maneuver, even when it is circumscribed by mandates.

One of the professional roles that teachers play is that of designer. To a greater or lesser extent (as enabled or constrained by mandates), all teachers have the opportunity to design the experiences their students will have in their classes. As curricular designers, your decisions are informed by the past and oriented toward future objectives. You have the opportunity to create the learning that will be experienced by you and your students.

This chapter describes the planning phase of the Lesson Study cycle, giving suggestions for how to choose a focus for your research lesson and how to design a lesson that is productive for both your Lesson Study team and, most important, for the students who experience it.

COLLECTIVE AGENCY AND INNOVATION

Collaborative planning is a chance to exercise collective agency, acting together in the best interest of students. As you plan during Lesson Study, you imagine innovative possibilities, choosing learning experiences that will resonate with the students in your classrooms. Instead of feeling constrained by requirements, you can see directives as creative challenges. Working with colleagues, you will generate novel ideas that you may have missed when planning on your own. Collaboration makes us nimbler and more resourceful.

When Bethani, Sarah, and Avery, preservice teachers at Old Wire, were planning a 1st-grade geometry lesson on the defining attributes of shapes, they brainstormed together about what might capture their students' interest in the topic. After discussing possible connections to the construction jobs that some of their students' parents worked, Bethani described her students' interest in art. They googled abstract art and found images that included geometric shapes and patterns. Bouncing ideas off one another, they planned an opening activity for their lesson that engaged their students' creative interests in their mathematical learning. Collaborative synergy enhanced their planning.

As you work with colleagues during Lesson Study, you come together around a shared question of practice. A common focus supports productive learning conversations.

Of course, there will be times during collaborative work when you won't feel this synergy, when you feel weighed down by the group instead of buoyed up by them. Look inward first and ask if now is your time to pull harder. In well-functioning groups, there is usually an ebb and flow of leadership: You take up the slack when I am having a hard day, and I'll do the same for you. Give when you can, and it will come back to you again. This is part of an effective collaborative process. As your group takes up this rhythm, sharing leadership in formal and informal ways, you will sustain synergy and maintain productivity. You can translate challenges into shared action as you see yourself and others in more generous ways (Newkirk, 2017).

CREATING A VISION FOR THE LESSON

An important aspect of Re*Visioning* through Lesson Study is that the research lesson is jointly constructed and of value to all group members. This provides a shared vision that gives energy for the hard work of planning. As team members plan together, the research lesson becomes not yours or mine but ours. This is also important later, during observation and debrief. The teacher being observed will be more confident in knowing that it is not her lesson being scrutinized, but rather the response of students to jointly designed learning activities. Observing team members bring a different attitude when they are looking to see how their collaboratively planned lesson is working with a particular group of students.

To have this shared vision, the Lesson Study cycle needs a focus that has urgency for everyone involved. Using or creating a unit of study situates the research lesson meaningfully within other work. Having time and opportunity to sketch out a whole unit together before diving into the research lesson is preferred, but when time is constrained, the group can develop a shared vision for a single lesson. This laser-sharp research focus can be powerful.

A Focus for the Work

Lesson Study creates opportunities to reflect, think deeply about new approaches, and plan for future use. Your team can build in time to brood over the challenges that vex you, to consider solutions, and to contemplate a strategy you've read about but haven't yet tried.

Effective planning starts with wondering. At the beginning of the Lesson Study cycle, your team reads and plans together, locking in on a problem of practice to investigate. As you plan the lesson, consider the needs of both students and teachers. Teachers' authentic wonderings create and sustain genuine inquiry. Such conversations stem from a place of curiosity, where questions are posed in the spirit of exploration versus advice or judgment.

When the Lesson Study topic stems from a current dilemma, attention is focused and teachers' learning is more fruitful. This focus might emerge from a review of data, from your current work, or from ongoing conversations about teaching and learning.

Data-Based Focus. As you consider a focus for your Lesson Study work, your group may want to consider student work, formative assessments, and results from standardized tests. This was the case during my Lesson Study work at Parker Elementary School. The district had already targeted writing as the area that needed to improve to move the school off of Turnaround status. For our first cycle of Lesson Study, we looked at a recent rubric-based formative assessment, where students' low scores on organization of writing attracted our attention. Their 5th-grade students were in the process of writing an animal report, so the lesson on organization, described in the Introduction, was a good fit, both from the perspective of assessment data and from the perspective of their current writing instruction. Standardized and formative assessment data provided a clear focus for our lesson.

Curriculum-Based Focus. Our initial focus on writing organization at Parker could also be seen as a curriculum-based focus. When we were planning our research lesson, students were in the midst of gathering facts about animals for their reports. The next logical step was for them to think about how to organize that information in their own writing. So, from a curriculum perspective, our focus on organization made sense.

Choosing a Lesson Study focus based on the what's next in your lesson plans or in the district's scope and sequence documents isn't a copout, but rather a recognition that any lesson can provide an opportunity for rich learning. As you study state standards and district curriculum guides, topics that invite inquiry will stand out. Your team can sketch out a series of lessons and determine which seems best for the deep dive—the rich inquiry of Lesson Study. You can consider how that lesson fits with a series of lessons or unit. As you review upcoming content, you might ask:

- Which topics have been difficult to learn or teach in the past?
- Is there content that students have not found interesting?
- Are there skills that students have not learned well in the past?

Lesson Study creates the opportunity to take a close look at generic curriculum materials and figure out how to make them work for the particular students sitting in your classrooms. The teachers' manual can become a starting place for collaborative inquiry.

Pedagogy-Based Focus. Another way to choose a focus for Lesson Study is by considering pedagogical approaches that you want to work on. Like me, you have probably had professional development experiences that left you with a desire to try something new. Or you have read an article or book that inspires you. Lesson Study can provide the collegial support for you to put those ideas into practice.

That was the case for two 4th-grade teachers in a Lesson Study group. Diana and Andi had attended trainings about Cognitively Guided Instruction (CGI) for teaching mathematics. Diana was especially excited about this method (see Carpenter, 2014). She liked the idea of building on students' intuitive approaches to expand their mathematical understanding. Andi wasn't so sure; she had seen the benefits of explicit instruction with her students, but she was willing to give the new ideas a try. So, together, they planned a lesson on solving multistep problems that used the CGI approach. Through participating in the Lesson Study process, both Diana and Andi became more confident with supporting students in constructing their own approaches to problem solving.

A pedagogy-based focus can work well with cross-disciplinary teams. For example, an unlikely combination of two math teachers and an English teacher were interested in collaborating through Lesson Study. These middle school teachers chose close reading as a common focus. They debated about whether their jointly constructed lesson should focus on vocabulary or visualizing. Eventually, they decided that focusing on instructional strategies that helped students construct visual images would deepen their pedagogical knowledge and their students' learning. They chose different passages to use, but their teaching strategies were the same. The math teachers chose word problems that allowed students to practice the mathematical strategies they'd been working on. The English teacher selected paragraphs from the novel they were reading. During the lesson, all of the teachers did think-alouds describing for students how details from the text helped them construct visual images of what they were reading. All three teachers felt the lesson supported students' understanding, and the teachers described how working with colleagues from another discipline strengthened their own learning. Taking a pedagogy-based focus for your Lesson Study could give you confidence to try a new approach.

Determining the Lesson Study Focus

The decision of what to focus on for your Lesson Study is an important one. You are going to invest a lot of time and effort into this process, so it needs to be one you can really sink your teeth into—something you all genuinely care about. And whenever a group of teachers comes together, they bring multiple passions and concerns. Narrowing from lists of ideas to a single focus can be a challenging process.

If a joint interest doesn't readily surface, I've found that the sequence of individual brainstorming followed by group deliberation helps. Here's an idea to try:

Each individual has a stack of sticky notes. For 3 minutes, everyone silently lists ideas for a possible focus, one idea per sticky (that 3rd minute lasts forever, but often that's when the best ideas emerge!). Now everyone has a bunch of possibilities. Taking a few more moments of silence, everyone sticks their ideas on the wall. Without talking, everyone starts moving the stickies into groups, putting similar ideas together. If you don't like where a note got placed, you can move it again. This process continues until everyone steps back, feeling satisfied with the groupings. Now the silence can be broken. Together, label each group of notes. If there is one group that is much larger than the others, you may have just found your Lesson Study focus! Have a seat and talk about that possibility as a group.

Alternatively, I sometimes chart the stickies, starting with one person listing their ideas, then adding only new ideas from the second person, but putting a checkmark next to any they had that were similar to the first. Joint interests again rise to the surface.

Whether you use one of these procedures or just sit and chat until you've figured it out, it's important that the focus you settle on for your Lesson Study cycle is one in which everyone is invested. Coming together around shared questions brings energy to the work.

Lesson Study as Action Research

Once you've found a focus that is really worth your time, you're ready to delve into the work. Lesson Study is action research guided by a collaborative process for inquiry. Action research "is a disciplined process of inquiry conducted by and for those taking the action. The primary reason for engaging in action research is to assist the 'actor' in improving and/or refining his or her actions" (Sagor, 2000, p. 3).

The idea of conducting research may sound intimidating, but in your work as a teacher, you are a researcher day in and day out. You bring research questions with you to school every day: What will help Tyler move to the next level? How can you motivate your 9th-graders after lunch? What will challenge those students who always finish early? Lesson Study brings a structured process for finding answers to your most burning questions. It formalizes your research.

A preliminary step, before the action of action research, is finding out what is already known about your topic of focus. This is the study phase of the Lesson Study cycle. Although a lot of collective wisdom resides in the heads of those in your group, you'll also want to consult other resources as you begin planning. If you work just with what is in your heads, you won't expand possibilities, and you won't learn as much.

Professional literature, curriculum guides, and teachers' manuals can inform your work. You may also want to call on subject-matter specialists, like instructional coaches or university faculty. Tap into the resources of professional organizations. Don't get caught up in trying to invent something new and creative. Your focus isn't on originality; it is on finding what will work best. Ideas that others have found useful are a good starting place. Investigating research and best practices ensures that you won't feel stuck as you face the blank lesson plan.

Like an accordion, the investigation phase of Lesson Study can expand or contract to suit the available time, the gravity of the question under consideration, and the investment you'll be putting into results.

During the 4th-grade math Lesson Study on multistep problems described earlier, Diana, Andi, and I looked at the conclusion section of several research articles about math instruction. Then we spent more time with an article written for teachers called "Orchestrating Discussions" (Smith, Hughes, Engle, & Stein, 2009) that laid out a model for using student responses to teach key mathematical ideas. This article aligned with the CGI training the teachers had attended, and it provided a helpful step-by-step process for getting started. The model guided our thinking as we planned and taught the research lesson. It helped us collect convincing evidence about the learning that occurred.

Perhaps the most important information you'll collect to guide your planning is data about your own students. A quick pretest, without any preliminary instruction, lets you know where students are. Their understanding right now about the topic, or their current ability to use the skill you've targeted, will determine your starting place for instruction. Once you know where they are, you know what to plan.

As an action researcher, you will take what you have learned about your focus and prepare to put it into action. Your own students are the intended audience for your results; your findings will guide your future practice.

Questions That Support Effective Planning

As you sit down together to plan the lesson that will be observed, you bring your own experience, ideas you have gleaned from other sources, and a clear starting point based on your students' present understanding. It makes sense to use the lesson plan format that you're used to, especially if you are required to turn it in to your administrator. Below are some questions that can guide your planning process. Jot down notes about your team's responses to these questions, and let them guide you as you fill in the blanks on your lesson plan.

- What is the lesson's objective? What important understandings do students need to develop? What do you want them to know and be able to do?
- In the past, what has been challenging about teaching this skill or topic?
- Based on your research and experience, what different approaches might be used to achieve these objectives?
- How does this lesson fit within the learning progression for this topic? How does it build on past learning? How does it set the stage for future learning?
- What do students already know?
- What misconceptions might students have?
- What might make the lesson motivating for students? How does it connect to students' cultures, interests, and needs?
- How can the lesson build on the current classroom culture and context?
- What structures and routines are in place that might support the learning?
- What materials will support student learning? What content, manipulatives, graphic organizers, and so forth might be beneficial?
- What key questions will be asked?
- How will the wording of problems and instructions appropriately support students without overscaffolding?

You can consider all, or just a few, of these questions to get the conversation about the lesson going. The template in Appendix B might also be helpful in guiding your planning conversation. As you plan, your focus should be on student thinking: How will you support it, and what will you see and hear as evidence of learning?

ReVisioning: Planning to See Student Thinking

How do you define learning? In your definition, you would probably include something about thinking. Bingham and Conner (2015) say that learning "changes what we know and builds on what we do" (p. 32). The combination of knowing and doing creates powerful learning.

When planning lessons for observation, you and your team will want to emphasize what teacher observers will see and hear. Knowing that you'll all have your eyes on students during the lesson, you want the observers to have plenty to see. Because the thinking that goes on inside students' heads can't be seen, you will want to include learning strategies that make thinking visible as you plan for Lesson Study. During the observation, team members will collect data about students' thinking so that the lesson's effectiveness can be evaluated. The gauge for effectiveness is how well students learn, based on evidence from what they do, say, and write.

What Students Do. Learning by doing doesn't just mean grand simulations and hands-on-real-artifacts experiences (although those activities certainly qualify). You don't have to be grandiose to have students learn by doing. You can keep things simple. For example, having students sort words or objects (according to categories of their own choosing) tells us a lot about their thinking. When they act out a book chapter they've just read, students demonstrate their comprehension. When they provide photo evidence of a science concept, we see what they understand. When young students stomp the syllables in a word, the rhythm tells us if they've got it. Not only does a "doing" approach give observing teachers a gauge for student thinking, it deepens students' learning.

I hear, and I forget. I see, and I remember. I do, and I understand. (Chinese Proverb)

What Students Say. As students talk and listen to one another, understanding develops. Peter Johnston, in *Choice Words* (2004), says that language "is not merely representational (though it is that); it is also constitutive" (p. 9). This means that words build something: They build understanding. As teachers listen in on student conversations, they collect evidence of students' depth of understanding.

An activity like Four Corners, where students go to a specified spot in the room based on their opinion, includes meaningful conversation. When students talk with a partner about what they see, think, and wonder (Fontichiaro, 2010), they are thinking deeply and making their thinking visible. When they talk with you as you confer during independent work time, students' words are a window to their understanding. Vygotsky (2012) suggests that by giving students practice in talking with others, we give them frames for thinking on their own. We also give ourselves frames for reflecting on instruction.

What Students Write. Although less interactive than doing and talking, writing is another beneficial way for students to build and demonstrate their understanding. Quick writes and exit tickets are formative assessments that get thinking on paper. When students explain their answers or describe their process in a math problem, they clarify their own thinking. Write-Pair-Share gives the opportunity some students need to prepare for conversation. Short sprints of writing can be beneficial during an observed lesson.

Long writing assignments give students a chance to flesh out ideas and elaborate on what they know, and that can play a useful role in the Lesson Study process. As you and your team look at what students have written, it helps you choose a focus for upcoming instruction. However, because that evidence is mostly available after the fact, it's not necessary to have an observation focused on students' production of such pieces.

During writing, students' minds are very active, and there are still some opportunities to observe (more about that in Chapter 5), but since there is not as much obvious activity, a lesson that includes mostly writing isn't appropriate for the observed lesson. Planning for some writing during the observed lesson is fine if that is what makes sense for students' learning progression.

As you and your team plan for what students will do, say, and write, build in opportunities for student self-assessment. What students tell you about their learning during the lesson will be a good indication of its success.

PREDICTIVE PLANNING

After you have fleshed out a lesson that includes opportunities to see student thinking, you can take the time, with your Lesson Study colleagues, to predict what those learning experiences will look like in action. Predictive planning will allow you to be preemptive, to replace weak areas in the lesson with stronger ones before enacting the plan. By anticipating student responses, you are also able to respond more effectively in the moment, to clarify concepts and correct confusion.

For example, during a middle school math Lesson Study in Berryville, teachers predicted that students would make calculation errors when working through the word problems. Because they anticipated that using the wrong operation might cause these calculation problems, teachers decided to emphasize how to choose the correct operation during their opening discussion. Their preemptive planning fended off student confusion. When it came time to teach the lesson, the teacher was tuned in for students who were confused about which mathematical operation to use. Her awareness had been heightened that this might be a concern.

Because Berryville teachers asked, "How do we anticipate that students will respond?," they proactively considered potential student confusion. Before you finish the planning phase, be sure to ask this question. Envisioning what student thinking will look like allows for re*Visioning* even before the lesson is enacted.

Reflect and Respond

1. *Read* and annotate the following quote:

> If we work just in our own heads and with familiar textbooks, we won't get anything new. Knowledge and perspectives from outside the group—in the form of research studies, high-quality curriculum, regional or university-based content specialists, and so forth—may greatly enrich a team's learning.
>
> —Lewis & Hurd, 2011, p. 46

Reflect & Respond: Think of a time when an outside perspective strengthened your work with a team. What did it add that had been missing? Why was this helpful?

2. *Read or watch* one of the following:

- https://prosky.co/careerbuzz/articles/how-to-be-a-great-team-player/
- https://tinyurl.com/Ch4-Scripted
- https://tinyurl.com/Ch9-Visible-Thinking

Reflect & Respond:

- How do the ideas in one of the above items relate to collaborative lesson planning?

3. *Read* the following quote:

> In preparing for battle I have always found that plans are useless, but planning is indispensable.
>
> —Dwight D. Eisenhower in Blair, 1957, p. 4

Reflect & Respond: Leaving the battle metaphor aside, how does Eisenhower's quote relate to your experience with lesson planning?

Self-Assess: Review the list in the section "Questions That Support Effective Planning." Put a star by one question that focuses on an area you want to get better at and make a plan for doing so.

CHAPTER 5

Observation
The Eyes Have It

A carefully planned research lesson gives rise to an effective observation. This chapter describes the observation phase in the Lesson Study process, including pre-observation planning, the importance of objective observation, and the value of having multiple teachers observing a lesson.

Observations are an experience ripe with prospects for instructional improvement, but they are infrequently included in professional development activities. Although teachers have years of experience observing from the student's seat, this apprenticeship of observation (Lortie, 1975) is a limited front-stage view, without consideration of teachers' decisionmaking and students' responses. During Lesson Study, observation attends to these aspects.

Observing your research lesson in action sharpens your attention to student learning and broadens your instructional repertoire. Observation supports inquiry and provides opportunities to develop your teaching craft. "Closed classroom doors will not help us educate all students to high levels" (City, Elmore, Fiarman, & Teitel, 2009, p. 3). The teacher who opens her doors for lesson observation also benefits, gaining multiple perspectives and increased information as she goes public with her practice.

ANOTHER PAIR OF EYES

Teaching and learning are complex processes, so the more eyes we have on the work, the better! Lesson Study provides opportunity to witness the multifaceted teaching/learning relationship. Whether you are teaching the lesson or observing, you will benefit from the increased perspectives provided.

For the Observer

Those who observe the research lesson are freed from the ongoing, intensive brainwork of on-the-spot decisionmaking. As an observer, you don't have to worry about what Marcus on the other side of the room is doing or get materials ready for what will come next in the lesson. You can give your energy to watching and listening. As Shelley Harwayne (2000) describes, observers have the chance to drive in the slow lane. It is a luxury to be able to choose where you will focus your attention, deciding what you will attend to and when. Observation during Lesson Study is a 3D experience. You look at the big picture and then lean in to look more closely. You have the chance to be selective about your observations, so you can give your full attention to how two students interact, then watch another student's struggle and ultimate triumph as she puzzles through a problem. You can look at the specific, then lift your gaze to see what others are doing, to note the arrangement of the room and how the choreography of the lesson is playing out. You see how and where the nuances of planning and the realities of learning come together. These are the benefits of being an observer.

For the Observed

In order for this rich observation to occur, someone will step forward to teach the research lesson. This is often a role that rotates among the group. You might have had your name randomly drawn to be the first to teach, or you might have volunteered because you had a strong vision for the lesson or because you were willing to take the risk. Charity, an experienced teacher at Stilwell High who had held many leadership positions, said, "I'm just not comfortable with other adults in the room." Tasha, the newest teacher on the team, stepped forward. Perhaps a new generation of teachers is breaking the long tradition of teacher isolation and becoming more comfortable taking practice public. Whatever the situation, if your group is new to the Lesson Study process, there may be some trepidation about being the first to be observed. Rest assured, there are structures in place to keep the process safe.

If you are preparing to be observed, remember that you will be teaching a lesson that has been collaboratively planned. Your group will think of the lesson as *our* lesson, and they will be watching students to see whether the activities you have created together generate student learning. The lesson you have planned is student-centered, so their focus will be on kids. Yes, colleagues will also make note of your spontaneous interactions with students and the shifts you make to the lesson plan, because these will provide valuable opportunities for discussion and learning. Your colleagues will be thinking about their own learning rather than focusing on what you should learn from the experience. You will never play to a friendlier audience!

Still, you may feel uneasy. You know that your students' behavior is unpredictable and that learning is an untidy process that doesn't ever go exactly as planned. Fortunately, your colleagues have had these same experiences. Superstar teachers like Professor Keating (Robin Williams) in *Dead Poets Society* are fictional characters that provide unrealizable models. Recognize that you may be holding yourself to a standard that no one else expects. Your colleagues know that real teaching and real learning are messy and imperfect.

Anxieties and hesitations arise because teaching publicly entails risk. As Thomas Newkirk says in his book *Embarrassment* (2017), "Any act of learning requires us to suspend a natural tendency to want to appear fully competent" (p. 10). Yes, you are making yourself vulnerable, but that is the "irreducible, unavoidable condition for learning" (p. 10). In the case of Lesson Study, the learning that occurs is for you, your students, and your colleagues. It is worth the risk. So embolden yourself and be vulnerable, and you will be amazed at the learning that occurs. You and your colleagues will gain a truer, more realistic picture of success.

BEFORE THE OBSERVATION

Observation day should include time immediately before the lesson to prepare, time in the classroom to teach and observe, and ample time to debrief (usually 2.5–3 hours total, depending on the length of the lesson; see Chapter 2 for suggestions on scheduling and classroom coverage).

Transformative learning takes time, and teachers have barely a chance to catch their breath during the regular school day. Lesson Study observations provide the thinking space needed for teacher learning. Appendix C includes a sample agenda for this time together, prepared by the 5th-grade Literacy Lesson Study team at Berryville Intermediate School (you'll read about their Lesson Study in Chapter 9).

Effective observation starts with wondering. During the pre-observation meeting, revisit the questions that guided your planning. Discuss what you are wondering about now. Will students grasp the concepts as intended? Will they find the work interesting? You may want to chart the group's questions so you can revisit them during your debrief meeting. You'll also want to review the lesson plan with an eye toward what to watch for.

Reviewing the Lesson

In their helpful book, *Lesson Study: Step by Step* (2011), Lewis and Hurd recommend that before the observation, teachers consider the planned learning activities, how they anticipate students will respond to these activities, and what they want to be sure to notice each step of the way. As a group, you may want to record these ideas in three columns on a large piece of chart paper, as shown in Figure 5.1, the pre-observation chart for a 3rd-grade lesson on fractions.

Before the lesson, the 3rd-grade teachers in this Lesson Study team talked briefly about each learning activity. For example, they discussed how Staci, who was teaching the lesson, would begin by using a balance scale and modeling clay to demonstrate equivalency. They jotted this in the chart under "Ss (students) Learning Activities" (see Figure 5.1). Would students recognize that the scale would still balance when Staci broke the clay on one side into two pieces? Talking it through, Candice suggested it would be helpful to have students make a prediction; they added "T (teacher) ask to hypothesize" to the "Anticipated Ss and T Responses" column. Candice and Samantha, the teachers who would be observing, wanted to be sure to note how many students predicted the scale would balance (thumbs up) and how many thought it wouldn't (thumbs down). They added this to the chart in the left column, under "Pts. (points) to Notice." As teachers thought their way through the lesson using the three-column chart, they hypothesized about students' responses and made a plan for what to notice.

When you simulate the lesson in your mind during your pre-observation meeting, you imagine how students will respond to your questions. You consider processes students will use when the teacher poses a problem. You realize missteps that may be taken along the way. You think about how the lesson might be adjusted if students respond this way or that.

This is also the time to stop and think about individual students and how the funds of knowledge they bring to the classroom will support their learning. Thinking through the 3rd-grade lesson on fractions, teachers wondered: Will Cindy, whose mother makes and sells baked goods, think about measuring cups? Will Marshall think of his uncle's carpentry tools? During your pre-observation meeting, you'll also want to anticipate how language and culture might impact students' responses to the learning activities. Plan to make note of these things, because it will help you adjust the lesson, improve its effectiveness, and apply new understandings in future planning.

When the Lesson Study team thinks the lesson through from the students' point of view, the one teaching is more prepared to support students' learning, and those who are observing are more prepared to make note of that learning. These anticipations prepare everyone for a more productive experience.

Making a Plan to Collect Evidence

The "points to notice" column on your pre-observation chart will guide your focus (see Figure 5.1), but it is also helpful to think beforehand about the structure you'll use for note-taking. You'll want to capture as much information as possible. Some teachers like to use two-column notes: what the teacher says/does in one column and what the students say/do in another. Others just write as fast as they can, trying to get exact words and notice actions and even facial expressions. I find it's helpful to draw lines in my notes to separate parts of the lesson. This helps me remember what was happening when I return to my notes later.

In addition to this free-flow, capture-everything approach, it can be helpful to have more structured tools for observation. For example, checkmarks on a

Figure 5.1. Pre-Observation Chart for a 3rd-Grade Lesson on Fractions at Old Wire Elementary School

Ss Learning Activities	Anticipated Ss + T responses	Pts. to Notice (evaluation)
T models equivalency using balance scale	-Ss will comment that they are obviously the same -T- body lang. okay + call out	-Who is convinced - Clap? (correct + incorrect minds) -Correct hypotheses?
-Ss work independently to solve problem in their quadrant	-T- Ask to hypothesize -Ss challenged, "Too hard" -T- by self? -Let them struggle -Fix later -Confused + too easy -Diff. exit slip	-Do kids persevere -What strategies are they using
-Ss explain their strategy to small group		
-Ss choose favorite from group	-Not 1 dominating -All share in sequence Pick the "smart kids"	-Does everyone talk about strategy -Smart or popular? Who gets picked?
-T chooses examples to share whole group. Ss "teach" strategy to group:	-May be t-ed or not -Ss are used to sharing -Ss will want to share -open to mistakes	-How other Ss are responding to S-teacher
-Ss ask S "teachers" ?'s	-Always ask "How" + "Why" -Ss will struggle explaining their thinking -T will be quiet	-Do they seem ready to try their strategy -Do they make room
-Ss complete exit slip	-3/4 + 5/6 -T will differentiate	for new strategies in their own strategies used?

seating chart can denote who responds (especially helpful since the observers may not know students' names). You might also design note-taking tools that align with specific goals for the lesson. For example, observers could draw arrows on the seating chart to show the flow of dialogue if a goal is to build student-to-student discussion, or a checklist could be created to note specific problem-solving approaches in math.

Sometimes it's helpful to divide and conquer. During a lesson on punctuation at Stilwell High, students worked in small groups to construct paragraphs from unpunctuated phrases. Each member of the Lesson Study team was assigned a group to follow as students moved from table to table to find their new scrambled-paragraph challenges. This allowed for interesting comparisons during the debrief as we talked about different approaches groups had taken for the task. Alternatively, each team member could have watched one station, reporting later on how groups responded to that task.

Planning in advance for how you will document the lesson is important. Be prepared—lessons unfold rapidly! There is so much to make note of, and you don't want to miss important moments. For practice beforehand, you might watch part of a lesson video and practice taking notes. (YouTube is full of such videos. See the suggestions in Appendix D.) Make the practice relevant by searching for a video related to your lesson. Scripting for a few minutes will prepare you for your authentic observation experience.

Even after you've become more experienced at note-taking, it's important to take a few minutes before the observation to plan for data collection (refer to the pre-observation agenda in Appendix C). A good plan for capturing data supports an effective postobservation debrief.

Expectations for Observers

Being a classroom observer requires a shift in patterns. You are used to being the one facilitating the learning, but now you will take a different role. Because this more passive stance is unusual for the teachers in your group, it is worth taking time to review expectations before heading to the classroom (refer to Appendix C). Below are a few recommendations to keep in mind. It's also helpful for students to be aware of these norms. A quick introduction by the teacher will do the trick.

Do Not Talk. Do not talk to one another, to students, or to the teacher. Later, there will be time to discuss what was seen and heard, but talking during the lesson is a distraction that influences the flow of the lesson you've so carefully constructed. When observers talk to one another, both the students and their teacher have an uncomfortable sense that they are being talked about. It doesn't matter that you are saying something good; it is still an unwelcome disruption.

If an observer talks with a student, once again the usual classroom dynamic is disrupted. Not going to a student with a raised hand, even if they look to you for support, feels awkward. But it is necessary if you want to know what the lesson looks like under typical circumstances. Similarly, avoid talking with the one who is teaching. She needs her full faculties for the important work she is doing!

Lean in to Listen. Even though you don't want to distract, you do want to hear what is happening, even during partner talk or small-group discussions. So get close. As you can see in Figure 5.2, one of the observers (Cherise, in darker scrubs) is right in the thick of things! The teacher is close by, helping a student, but Cherise is paying keen attention to the students around her, ready to make notes about what she is seeing and hearing as students review a story, finding textual evidence about character traits to share with their partners.

Even though you may be in close proximity to students during the observation, you'll want to avoid eye contact with them so students don't start talking with you. Sometimes I sidle up to a group and stand with my back to them; I can hear just fine, and they are not distracted by my presence. If my eyes are on the bulletin board instead of on them, their conversation is more natural. Once students become comfortable having other adults in the room, you can be less cautious about your intrusion.

Shift Your Focus. Even if the group has decided to divide responsibilities so that you are watching a particular group of students, it is helpful to look up

Figure 5.2. Observation of a Research Lesson

and observe how that group's participation fits with the others. You'll want to take in as much as possible about the learning that is occurring.

Take Nonevaluative Notes. Before heading to the classroom, remind yourself that your notes should be objective. Writing "Good partner talk" in your notes will give you little to discuss during the debrief; if instead you write, "S: I use measuring cups when I'm cooking," you'll have more fodder for learning. Remind yourself to write what you see and hear, not your evaluation of those observations. (Note: Using abbreviations, like T for teacher and S for student, helps you capture more, faster.)

With these reminders in place, you are ready to observe!

THE OBSERVATION: SEEING WITH NEW EYES

Observation is a tool for instructional change. Whether you are a novice or a veteran, watching others teach gives you new perspectives. In my work with preservice teachers, I often show short video clips of teaching to demonstrate a practice. Later in the semester, I have student teachers show videos of themselves, highlighting things that are going well. These short recordings are useful, but, unfortunately, they may create unrealistic expectations, since they tend to be carefully clipped to show the parts of the lesson when everything is going as planned.

In contrast, observation during Lesson Study lets you see the real deal. You might be relieved to see that things aren't perfect. But instead of focusing on the imperfections, you will take careful note of the learning that is going on. As you lean in to listen, you will learn about students' clarity and their confusion. Being an observer will help you see with new eyes. The quote from Marcel Proust (1974) in the Introduction takes on special relevance as you step into the classroom to observe: "The real voyage of discovery consists not in seeking new landscapes, but in having new eyes" (p. 131). When you come with eyes ready to learn about practice, you will make discoveries within the familiar landscape of your colleague's classroom.

Members of a Lesson Study team are not there to critique the teacher, but to learn from watching him and from watching his students navigate the complexities of teaching and learning. Teaching is professional practice. *Think* about that word's multiple definitions. As a noun, *practice* means professional business. As a verb, it means to perform repeatedly in order to improve. When you step into a colleague's classroom for an observation, realize that you are seeing practice. View with generous eyes, recognizing that you are seeing experimentation, not perfection. Learn through the lens of respect. Hopefully, the lesson will not go exactly as planned. It bears repeating that if the outcome is exactly what was expected, you will not really learn anything—you will just reinforce what you already knew!

Seeing Through Students' Eyes

During an observation, take objective notes of what you see, hear, and notice. Be mindfully aware. Jon Kabat-Zinn (2003) defines *mindfulness* as "the awareness that emerges through paying attention, on purpose, in the present moment, and nonjudgmentally, to the unfolding of an experience" (p. 145). When we are mindful, we are open to new information and aware of more than one perspective. We pay attention to aspects of the environment that we might otherwise overlook. Being mindful helps us see more clearly and challenge moment-to-moment judgments.

From time to time during the lesson, purposefully pause, center yourself, and do a sense check, attending to all that is going on around you. Turn your head, shift your position. Experience the moment and carefully record your observations. You are responsible for bringing these notes to the debrief discussion. You will want to provide a trustworthy report.

Remember to scan from whole class to small group. Follow a child. Track transitions. Note the classroom environment, recording evidence of the tone and community. Jot down what time it is. During whole-group instruction, position yourself where you can see students' faces. Script conferences and interactions. Watch for ongoing assessment. Listen for the teacher demonstrating her own thinking processes. See and hear the nuances of student and teacher actions and interactions. Capture questions and responses.

Teachers often have the chance to review test scores or student work after the fact—fossilized learning. But when you observe, you see the living work of learning. Look closely at students and the work they are doing. Listen to what the teacher says and to how students respond. The classroom is a data-rich place. You'll want a thick description, so sharpen your senses. Your notes will lead to learning.

For example, when Allie, one of the 5th-grade teachers at Parker Elementary in our Lesson Study group, taught the lesson on vivid details (see Chapter 1), we noticed that when a student example was placed under the document camera, the students talked about specific words they liked. We jotted down those words and how the students responded.

As you take notes, be sensitive to the affective responses of students; this will give you clues about the fit between the lesson and your students' interests and culture. These details will also give you a sense of whether the lesson is successfully building on students' background knowledge. Notice students' "aha" expressions and their looks of confusion. For example, when observing a 3rd-grade math lesson at Old Wire Elementary School, the Lesson Study team noticed how confused students seemed when the teacher described elapsed time. When she connected the concept with their frequent question "How long until lunch?," lightbulbs went on and students were more engaged with the learning. Noticing students' affective responses helped the team realize the importance of making connections between lesson content and students' experiences.

During Lesson Study observations, your awareness of the unique attributes of each class and each student will increase because you are freed from teaching to focus on learning. When observing, you will want to be especially tuned to how context and culture are impacting students' responses. Make note of these, because it will help you adjust the lesson, improve its effectiveness, and apply new understandings in future planning.

Seeing Is Believing

Watching an unfolding lesson through an outsider's lens helps observers slow it down and take it in. Teacher learning occurs alongside student learning as you see the ideas you have collaboratively planned brought to life.

As you observe, you will pause and think in different ways about your practice. Seeing a strategy work, especially in your own school, can nudge you in a new direction. Understanding can be changed through exposure to new information or even through looking at what you already know in a different way.

Patterson and Tolnay (2015) compare classroom observation to a ride in a glass-bottomed boat. In the way that a glass-bottomed boat helps us see life under the sea, being lesson observers gives us the chance to leave our familiar reef and see the underlife of learning. Like the glass-bottomed boat, lesson observation is a vessel; it can lead us to new understandings.

At a time when accountability systems equate observations with high-stakes evaluation, peer observation is a welcome change; this looking is about learning! We learn from what works and from frustrations and failures. As Roland Barth (2006) has said, "There is no more powerful way of learning and improving on the job than by observing others and having others observe us" (p. 11). Having a reference beyond our own practice helps us analyze, question, and build new understandings. Being thoughtfully observant during a lesson deepens our knowledge of best practice.

Technology provides the opportunity to easily collect video and audio records of a lesson, but this is second-best to actual classroom observation. When we observe, we step into the lesson. We feel the energy of the students. We experience the flow of time. We notice how the physical arrangement of the room and the use of materials support the learning. We absorb student and teacher interactions. We experience the lesson. Through observation during Lesson Study, we soak up ideas and sharpen our vision for student learning.

Seeing is believing. Observing our lesson in action opens the door to new possibilities. It shifts our expectations as we re*Vision* what is possible.

Reflect and Respond

---

1. ***Read*** and annotate the following quote:

   > It is clear that closed classroom doors will not help us educate all students to high levels. It is also clear that what happens in classrooms matters for student learning and that we can do more together than we can do individually to improve learning and teaching.
   >
   > —City et al., 2009, p. 3

   Reflect & Respond: How does opening classroom doors contribute to high levels of learning?

2. ***Read or watch*** one of the following:

   - https://www.educationworld.com/a_admin/admin/admin297.shtm
   - https://www.cultofpedagogy.com/open-your-door/
   - https://www.youtube.com/watch?v=c_W6tb35r3M

   Reflect & Respond:

   - How does Lesson Study support the described characteristics of effective peer observation?

3. **Read** the following quote:

> It's sometimes funny to watch some people doing something the wrong way but doing it confidently. Even more funny, they succeeded.
>
> —Beta, 2010, p. 27

Reflect & Respond: After considering this quote, what do you realize about your own preconceived notions? Have you experienced someone succeeding when you thought they were going about something the wrong way?

Self-Assess: How comfortable are you having peers observe your teaching? Rate yourself on a 1–4 scale, 1 = I am very uncomfortable to 4 = I am very comfortable having peers observe my teaching. Do you need to improve your comfort level? If so, how will you do it? If you are already very comfortable with peer observation, what helped you develop this attitude?

CHAPTER 6

Debrief
Deep Reflection and Lesson Re*Visioning*

What did you notice as you observed your team's research lesson in action? If the lesson did not go exactly as planned, differences between the imagined and the enacted lesson provide opportunities for reflection and learning.

During the observation, you gathered objective information. Now, after the observation, is the debrief, the time to put that information into action. It is the time to analyze, to figure out what worked and why, what didn't and why not. It is the time to be critical, remembering the definition of critical as involving skillful judgment. It is the time to re*Vision* your lesson and your practice.

Reflection and re*Visioning* occur during the debrief meeting, ideally held immediately after the lesson observation. Allow an hour so there's time to get below surface observations and think deeply. Follow-up meetings may be necessary to revise the lesson and complete the cycle (refer to the second half of Appendix C).

A DISPOSITION FOR REFLECTION

Professional development is effective when it encourages teachers to reflect on and discuss their students' thinking and learning (Whitcomb et al., 2009). The debrief session of Lesson Study provides this opportunity to engage with student thinking and to consider your students and your own daily work, to think about substance, content, and process (Franke, Carpenter, Levi, & Fennema, 2001).

Reflection is the act of recapturing one's experience, mulling it over, and evaluating it in order to learn about one's practice. Reflecting on practice (their own and that of others) encourages teachers to revisit instructional experiences and maximizes the construction of meaning (Matanzo & Harris, 1999; Schön, 1987). Reflection on practice is a critical step for improved instruction. It helps teachers move toward a more reasoned (less intuitive) stance, weighing evidence and clarifying goals.

As you and your team reflect on your research lesson, you will think through the learning process and deconstruct the instructional moves that made an impact. Through both individual and collaborative reflection, you will recognize areas that need strengthening, consider alternatives, and re*Vision* your teaching.

Individual Reflection

Immediately after the lesson observation, but before talking to one another, each group member should take time for individual reflection. Resist the urge to chat with one another about the lesson right away. Instead, stay silent while each of you reviews your notes so that you can highlight, underline, or put a star by anything that seems important.

Sometimes it might be helpful to have a reflection template specific to your lesson, such as the chart in Figure 6.1, created by Bethani Hoelzeman for the 1st-grade geometry lesson described in Chapter 4. Bethani felt that it would be especially helpful for her Lesson Study team to reflect on how students communicated their ideas, any misconceptions students expressed about attributes that define a shape, and evidence of their understanding about this concept. She also wanted them to note whether students made connections to prior knowledge or asked questions during the lesson. As teachers reviewed their notes at the beginning of the debrief session, they found relevant information and filled in their charts individually. Later in the debrief session, these insights helped them revise their lesson plan (for a before-and-after view of this plan, see Appendix E; a 5th-grade example is also included).

After reviewing your notes, take time for written personal reflection to synthesize these ideas and capture fleeting thoughts while they are still fresh. Think about what you have just seen and how it relates to your own teaching and learning. Challenge your judgments. Step back from instinctive responses and look deeper. Scan your mind for impressions and write them down. Notice your emotions and concerns. This reflective writing will increase your perceptiveness and discernment and support your reasoning.

Be sure to think about what went right in the teaching—strategies you would want to use again. Often, teachers' inclination is to reflect only on things they would change. While that is important, much can be learned from thinking about what went well. So, you'll need to make a point of taking an appreciative, strengths-based perspective when reflecting (He, 2009). As you temporarily set aside negative judgments, you'll gain insight about effective instruction.

Another thing to purposefully consider as you individually reflect is the culture and context of the observation classroom. While you write your reflection, revisit the classroom in your mind and note anything that stands out about the classroom context and students' cultures. Jot down your impressions about how these factors influenced students' learning and also any questions you have related to context, culture, and on-the-spot decisionmaking.

Figure 6.1. Individual Reflection Template for a 1st-Grade Lesson at Old Wire Elementary School, by Bethani Hoelzeman

Geometry—Shapes and Attributes—Observation	
Communicating Ideas	
Misconceptions	
Reasoning	
Defining vs. Nondefining (evidence of understanding)	
Connections Made to Prior Knowledge	
Questions	

Teachers who take time for mindful reflection are more likely to self-correct their own teaching skills (Amobi, 2005). Written reflection following the observation gives you the chance to consider the recent teaching in relation to past experiences. This initial writing can open opportunities for thinking deeply together during the debrief.

Collaborative Reflection

During Lesson Study, the debrief session provides authentic opportunities for teachers to share their work and problem-solve together as they explore perceptions and interpretations of the research lesson. You will create and sustain a collegial community and expand your teaching repertoire as you think together about student learning.

Because teachers spend most of their work week alone, in what educational sociologist Dan Lortie (1975) called "cellular isolation," you'll need to be intentional about collaborative reflection. Figure 6.2, "Tools for Listening and Responding," provides reminders for keeping conversations productive. These five Ps (pausing, paraphrasing, probing, presuming positive intentions, and paying attention) are guides for participants during

Figure 6.2. Tools for Listening and Responding

- Pausing: Pause before responding. Knowing you will pause, you can give your full attention to listening. The pause is your thinking time to process what you have heard.
- Paraphrasing: Briefly summarize what your colleague said. This demonstrates your attention and is a check for understanding. You can use a paraphrase starter like, "So, you're thinking . . . ."
- Probing: Ask for clarification or elaboration by using phrases such as "Please say more about . . . " or "I'm interested in . . . ." Responses to these probing questions make thinking more concrete.
- Presuming Positive Intentions: Assume that others' intentions are positive. Trust your colleagues.
- Paying attention to self and others: Stay aware of what is being said and how others are responding.

collaborative reflection. Using these tools supports dialogue, assists the group in hearing and understanding one another, and encourages collaborative decisionmaking.

Of course, these listening tools will only be useful if someone is talking! Balance listening with sharing during collaborative reflection. Put your own ideas on the table using phrases such as "Here is one idea . . ." or "Another consideration might be . . ." This language keeps the conversation open to additional suggestions. Both inquiring into the ideas of others and advocating for one's own ideas are important to productive dialogue.

Before beginning the discussion, it's especially important to remind yourselves, as observers, to be sensitive to the teacher who has generously invited you into her classroom for the research lesson. It takes courage for teachers to allow colleagues to observe instruction in action. Review the lesson with a respectful eye and eliminate "You should have" comments. This doesn't mean that the team can't chuckle together about a funny situation or puzzle over occasional chaos that may have ensued. But do this with an eye toward supporting your own learning and improving the lesson you have collaboratively designed. Honor the trust the observed teacher afforded when she opened her door to you.

As you reflect collaboratively on the research lesson, you increase your collective efficacy—your belief that what you do as teachers makes a difference for student outcomes. Collective teacher efficacy is strongly correlated with increased student achievement—it is three times more powerful and predictive of achievement than student motivation, socioeconomic status, or home environment and parental involvement (Hattie, 2012). Collaborative reflection builds principled knowledge that will guide your future instructional decisions (Franke et al.,, 2001). You will grow as a teacher and as a learner. You will get smarter together.

REFLECTION STARTS WITH DESCRIPTION

As you discuss the observed lesson with colleagues, you will want to begin with concrete descriptions of what was heard and seen. Rather than saying, "I liked how twelve students asked questions," you will share data that are free of value judgment, such as "I counted twelve students who asked questions." Nonjudgmental sharing of data grounded in what you have seen and heard will lead to rich discussions.

When you talk about the teaching, it may be tempting to describe things you see as matters of "style," especially when teaching differs from what you would have done. But describing teaching differences as matters of style trivializes our profession. Differences in instruction represent different approaches to our practice as teachers. Push beyond broad language to give specifics about what the observed teacher did. Talking about teaching as "style" attaches the teaching to the teacher, making it too personal to critique. Instead, you can say, "I noticed that when [the teacher] did _____, students _____." Describing differences will improve practice. Focusing your analysis on specific data that were collected keeps the conversation safe and helps you and your team dig deep into the art and science of teaching, making links between instruction and student learning.

Although you will sometimes talk about what you saw and heard the teacher do, the focus during the Lesson Study debrief is on students' responses. You already know what the teacher did (you have the broad strokes in your lesson plan). Insights about how students responded to the lesson will guide lesson re*Vision* and support instructional improvement. The skills you develop as keen observers during Lesson Study have broad benefits when they grow into your own classroom: As you teach, you come to notice and reflect more on your students than on your own actions.

Notice and Name

Peter Johnston (2004) reminds teachers to help students observe closely and look for patterns, noticing and naming what they see. Johnston suggests that this practice invites students to make sense of information. The same practice can be applied during the Lesson Study debrief conversation. By noticing and naming features of the research lesson, you learn more about elements of effective instruction.

Your noticings include recognition of the different ways students responded during the lesson and how these differences might relate to students' cultures. As you describe the lesson, consider how students' background knowledge and previous experiences influenced their learning. How did their values, beliefs, and attitudes come into play? Because you are observing colleagues with similar student populations, answers to these questions will have relevance in your own classroom.

During the debrief session, share your noticings by giving everyone in the group the opportunity to describe something they saw or heard and tell why it matters. Working your way chronologically through the lesson ensures that you don't miss important details. In Figure 6.3, notice the two new columns—"What did we notice?" and "Why is it important?" (Lewis & Hurd, 2011) that teachers added to the chart for their 3rd-grade lesson on fractions (described in Chapter 5). As you and the other team members add to the "What did we notice?" column of your own chart, using the sentence stem "I saw" or "I heard" will steer you away from evaluative comments. These notes are a way for you to record your thinking so that you can make inferences about effective instructional practice.

Ladder of Inference

Connecting objective noticings to statements of importance (What did I notice, and why is it important?) requires making inferences. These inferences signal aspects of effective instruction that transcend the specific lesson. Because your inferences will guide future instruction, you'll want to make sure they are well reasoned. The "Ladder of Inference," described by Chris Argyris (in Senge, 1990), can help.

Argyris's ladder describes steps that guide reasoning. Making inferences begins with filtering our experiences. This happened first while you were observing the research lesson and deciding what to include in your notes. You further filtered during individual reflection as you highlighted what was important. Even on this initial rung of the Ladder of Inference, you reap benefits by thinking with colleagues, because each of you will have filtered differently, highlighting varied aspects of the lesson.

After determining which aspects of the lesson you will analyze, you move to the next rung on the Ladder of Inference, interpreting what these observations mean. To do so, you apply assumptions about teaching and learning, which lead to conclusions. For example, in the "What did we notice?" column of Figure 6.3, you can see that some students verbalized their thinking when describing how they solved the fractions problem, that group members then asked clarifying questions, and that some students corrected their answers as a result of this discussion. This led the teachers of the Lesson Study team to the conclusion that students should be encouraged to explain their answers because this helps them correct errors (noted in the "Why is it important?" column).

According to Argyris's Ladder of Inference, teachers will develop beliefs based on their conclusions and then take actions that seem right based on these beliefs. To ensure that your conclusions are well founded, ask clarifying questions as ideas are put forward. Ask a colleague to "say more about that." The conversation will help your group to make meaning of what they have seen and deconstruct best practices, articulating how to adapt instructional

Figure 6.3. Debrief Chart for a 3rd-Grade Lesson on Fractions at Old Wire Elementary School

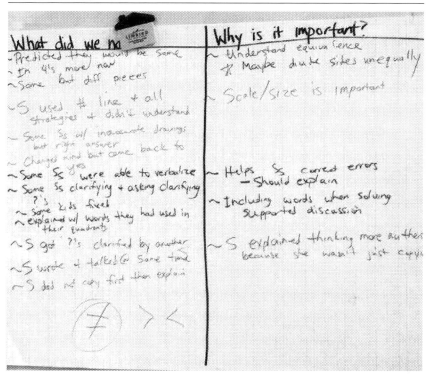

techniques to your own student population. Carefully connecting observations to conclusions will ensure that the beliefs you form and the actions you subsequently take are deliberate and justified.

RE*VISIONING* THROUGH APPRAISING AND APPRECIATING

Walking your way through the lesson again, adding your noticings and conclusions, helps you and your team re*Vision* the lesson. Re*Visioning* means perceiving it differently, creating another view. You are now more aware of important aspects of the teaching and learning involved. Your careful review of the observed lesson gives you insight about content and approaches and foresight about adjustments needed for your own classroom. Analysis from different perspectives helps you develop cognitive flexibility (Spiro & Jehng, 1990), allowing you to apply what you have learned to novel and unique situations.

Just as revising a piece of writing makes it clearer and more coherent, your lesson and your teaching will become stronger as you re*Vision* them.

Capture and develop the ideas you've discussed and re-create them for your own classroom. As you think about adaptations you will make to the lesson based on what you have learned, continue asking questions and reflecting on both successes and failures.

Recover and Discover

As your team's research lesson unfolded, there were, almost certainly, things that did not go as planned. These are golden learning opportunities! Unintended outcomes provide the chance to recover and discover.

Now is the time for all of you to use your critical judgment and think about what to discard and what to modify. You took some risks when you planned the lesson, using new ideas that you were unsure of. That is how we learn and grow. When things don't go as planned, we can view the activity as an approximation of success. It is a step in the direction of improvement. If you haven't uncovered something in the lesson that didn't work, look again; look harder. By uncovering weaknesses, you will find opportunities to strengthen the lesson.

Look at a place where the lesson came unhinged, where perhaps it overshot students' abilities. Process it with your colleagues and imagine it differently, making adjustments to the lesson plan. Having seen the lesson in action, you will have a clearer mental picture of what it could be, with modification. Ask:

- What if ... ?
- Would it be possible to ... ?
- If we [did this], then could students ... ?

See Figure 6.4 for a list of questions to consider during the debrief.

No matter how well the lesson went, there were students for whom the lesson went less well. Think about these students.

> That is what happened during the 3rd-grade fractions lesson mentioned in Chapter 5. Teachers noticed that Miguel, an English language learner, had trouble verbalizing his problem-solving process to the group. They also noticed that Miguel hadn't included any words when showing his work for how he solved the problem. Others had. The teachers wondered if supplying Miguel and other English language learners with a list of related math words would help them articulate their work. So they decided that on English language learners' copies of the problem, a word bank would be included to support explanation.

Looking closely at individual learning leads to additional differentiation of the lesson and new understandings of how culture and context influence

Figure 6.4. Questions to Ask During Debrief

- What did you notice as you observed your research lesson?
- Why is this important?
- What did we figure out while teaching this lesson?
- Why do you think that?
- How did students' values, beliefs, and attitudes come into play?
- What if . . . ?
- Would it be possible to . . . ?
- If we did [this], then could students do [that]?
- Would the lesson benefit from restructuring?
- Are there places where fine-tuning is needed?
- What changes should we make before teaching this lesson again?
- What should we keep?

instruction. It draws attention to variation within your own classroom and spurs ideas for responding to such variation.

During debrief, you will want to think both macro and micro as you re*Vision* your lesson. Would the lesson benefit from restructuring? Are there places where fine-tuning is needed? As you work through these ideas, be mindful of the feelings of the colleague who taught the research lesson. Remind yourself to be thoughtful and respectful in your conversations. Talk about the teaching rather than the teacher; most importantly, talk about the learning.

If you are the one who taught the research lesson, applaud yourself for being willing to take this risk. You are facilitating the learning of your group. You knew that trying something new meant potential awkwardness and partial success. You knew you might wobble (Garcia & O'Donnell-Allen, 2015). But you opened your door anyway. Vulnerability is "the irreducible unavoidable condition for learning" (Newkirk, 2017, p. 10).

As you talk through the lesson you taught, explain, but don't rationalize. You know your own students well and can offer insights about their responses, but to learn, you must overcome the tendency to want to appear fully competent. Remember that super-teachers are myths. Open yourself to new perspectives. Use the debrief to "drain setbacks of their emotionality" (Newkirk, 2017, p. 188) so that you can take a learning stance as you reflect on both successes and less successful aspects of the lesson.

Retaining Successes

As you review your list of conclusions, be sure to notice things that went well. Some of these were preplanned, but other insights became apparent during the unfolding of the lesson. Think about how to incorporate these insights into the lesson plan. For example, a conclusion drawn during the fractions lesson debrief, depicted in Figure 6.3, was that as students discussed the process they used to solve the fractions problem, it helped them to correct errors, especially when students asked their peers clarifying questions. Because of this insight, the team modified the lesson's directions for the small-group work. After "Each group member describes how they solved the problem," the teachers added the step, "Ask questions about what they did." Teachers wanted to be sure students were listening to and learning from one another.

When we lift something from the lesson that went well and hold it up for examination, we increase the chances that it will happen again. Noticing and naming successes settles them in our brains so that we can call them up again when the situation warrants. Our teaching toolkit gets bigger.

That's what happened when we celebrated the small-group work in the 3rd-grade fractions lesson described in Figure 6.3. Students found success as they worked a problem independently in their quadrant of a large sheet of bulletin board paper and then shared their process with others in their small group. The approach worked so well that teachers used it again, not only in math, but also in other academic areas.

As you look closely at a lesson, you will find many things that went right. Celebrate successes. They are the answer to the question, "What should we keep?"

RE*VISIONING* TEACHING AND LEARNING

As members of a Lesson Study team, we re*Vision* future lessons as we decide what to hang onto and what to change. When we compare the lesson with what we thought would happen, we learn about students and how context and culture influence their responses. When we ask, "What did we figure out while teaching this lesson?" and "Why do you think that?", we increase our understanding. When we ask, "What changes will we make before teaching this lesson again?", we refine our instructional repertoire. As we explore different perspectives, we learn about learning.

Learning has been described as a combination of accretion, tuning, and restructuring (Rumelhart & Norman, 1976). Teacher learning is no different. Accretion means a gradual accumulation. Each lesson taught, each lesson observed, adds a layer of growth as we recognize successful approaches. We also grow as we tune the specific lesson, making fine-grained adjustments, just as a mechanic's adjustments during a tune-up help the engine run more smoothly. Sometimes the research lesson gives us reason to dramatically change our teaching. Restructuring instruction is like an engine overhaul. Through accretion, tuning, and restructuring, the Lesson Study debrief supports instructional improvement that is responsive to our own needs and those of our students. I hope you'll be like Linda, the 5th-grade teacher at Parker Elementary, who, after the observation and debrief, said, "I love this! I am going to have to make some changes for my group, but seeing it helps me figure out what they're going to need."

Having collegial conversation after observation helps us reflect, make meaning of what we have seen, and take the learning deeper. Our inquiry is based on questions that arise during the lesson and during our discussion.

Because Lesson Study is inquiry-based, open-ended professional development, each teacher walks away with unique reminders or discoveries. At the conclusion of a literacy lesson debrief, the teachers in an elementary Lesson Study group shared these things they wanted to be sure to do:

- Provide explicit directions for activities and include varied activities for student engagement.
- Have students explain their thinking (verbal or written).
- Provide opportunities for students to talk to their peers as they learn new things.
- Think more in-depth and specifically about procedures and steps for activities.
- Plan, prepare, and understand the different ways students process information.
- Ask students to elaborate their answers.

Each teacher wrote her takeaway on a 3" x 5" card, and the teachers commented that they wanted to put the card where they would see it often, to remind them of their new vision for instruction.

The Lesson Study debrief provides a space to unpack experience and think about both the observable and the inner work of teaching. Teaching is complex and messy because you and your students are unique. Privileging examination of your own practice as a way to improve instruction values teachers and teaching and the work you do every day.

Reflect and Respond
---

1. **Read** and annotate the following quote:

> Often teachers' inclination is to reflect on everything that went wrong, what they forgot to say or do, and the ways they should have done better. Honest, candid reflection is certainly important; it helps us refine our craft. However, when I observe pre- or in-service teachers, I begin by asking them to describe everything that worked and that they would do again. If we don't take the time to do this, it's an afterthought, if ever a thought at all.
>
> —Lucas, 2017, p. 139

Reflect & Respond: Think of a lesson you recently taught or observed. What went right? How does reflecting on what went right help you?

2. ***Read or watch*** one of the following:

   - https://www.skillsyouneed.com/ps/reflective-practice.html
   - https://tinyurl.com/Ch6-Reflect-on-Failure
   - https://www2.usgs.gov/humancapital/ecd/professionaldevtools/LadderofInference.pdf

   Reflect & Respond:

   - How do the ideas in one of the above items relate to reflection after lesson observation?

3. ***Read*** the following quote:

   Life can only be understood backwards; but it must be lived forwards.
   —Søren Kierkegaard, 1843, p. 164

   Reflect & Respond: How can looking backwards on a lesson that has been taught improve future lessons?

   Self-Assess: Review Figure 6.2, "Tools for Listening and Responding." Put a star by one you want to get better at and make a plan for doing so.

PART III

REFINING THE FOCUS

CHAPTER 7

Building Understanding

At this point, you may have had a chance to experience one or two cycles of Lesson Study. With each cycle, the structure and protocols of Lesson Study become more familiar. Being freed from thinking about the routine, you are able to deepen your own learning. Predictability and consistency foster ingenuity. Chapters 7, 8, and 9 focus on understanding, flexibility, and responsiveness—concepts for your team to collectively wrap your minds around as you work toward continuous instructional improvement.

This chapter considers the instructional goal of building understanding and conceptualizes what understanding looks and sounds like during a lesson and in your own learning. Understanding, for both students and teachers, is a goal of Re*Visioning* through Lesson Study.

WHAT IS UNDERSTANDING?

When defining understanding, it is helpful to think first about what it is not. Understanding is not knowledge. It is not the ability to recall a storehouse of facts. It is not surface-level regurgitation of trivia. It is not repeating someone else's claim. Understanding is something you see and comprehend for yourself. You get the what and why of it. You don't just know facts, you make meaning of them, connecting them and using them.

Wiggins and McTighe (2005) describe understanding as multidimensional and complicated. Understanding is conceptual. It is made up of conclusions that are derived or grasped, not simply told or memorized. Understanding is deep. It includes inferences and insights, principles and generalizations that go beyond the obvious.

When you understand, you extend the information given and make meaning of your own. Understanding is insightful, nuanced, coherent, and thorough. When you understand, you can substantiate or justify. Understanding is a worthy goal, not easily achieved.

Understanding is built on knowledge—both content knowledge and procedural knowledge of how things are done. These forms of knowledge are building blocks for understanding. To understand, you must know, but you must do something with what you know to generate understanding.

Obtaining Understanding

Understanding is built, not acquired; worked for, not supplied. It is not heard or read but considered and deduced. When we understand, we don't borrow an expert opinion; we internalize an idea. Understanding can't be given to someone; they have to work for it themselves. The tuition of effort and diligence must be paid to own understanding.

If understanding is a goal for teachers and students, we must choose a learning path that leads to it. As teachers, when we want our students to understand, we plan learning experiences where students are active participants. They are meaning-makers, not meaning-takers. An answer that is given by the teacher isn't typically remembered for very long. An answer that is discovered is usually retained.

During Lesson Study, we intentionally plan learning activities that allow observers to see students' thinking. This is an important aspect of teaching for understanding. As you worked through previous Lesson Study cycles, you made sure learners were active. When learners are agentive in the learning process, rather than simply being acted upon, understanding is generated.

When understanding is the goal, classroom discussions go beyond recitation. Recitation allows a person to convey his understanding, but doesn't allow him to develop it (Newkirk, 2017). When teachers target understanding, they aren't looking for set answers. Classroom discussions (both whole-class and small-group) encourage exploratory talk that engages students with formulating, refining, and extending an idea. As you plan research lessons for Lesson Study, are you including opportunities for talking, thinking, and doing?

Similarly, when teachers have understanding as a goal for themselves, they aren't satisfied with being told someone else's answers about best practices. "Sit and get" PD won't do the trick. Like your students, you learn through doing, through discussing, and through self-deliberation. You start with professional knowledge, try it, think it through, and make it your own. Through this process, textbook knowledge becomes real understanding. Lesson Study provides this opportunity to be active in the learning process. Participants seek learning; they don't wait to be taught. If this is your attitude as you engage in Lesson Study, you will find your own answers.

Using Understanding

Understanding is useful because it helps us see and do things differently. It structures our knowledge and informs our actions. We demonstrate understanding as we explain and enact what we have learned.

Understanding can be evidenced through explanation. We can say what something means and why it matters. We aren't just recalling or repeating someone else's words; we have internalized ideas so that we can draw useful inferences, make connections between facts, and state conclusions in words of our own. We can defend a claim in the face of counterclaims because we have thought it through. We can give examples. We can provide interpretations that extend meaning. We understand various perspectives. We can say what we see differently.

Understanding enhances our ability to do. We demonstrate our understanding when we enact it through skillful performance. For a student studying fractions, this might look like being able to solve a problem in multiple ways and choosing the most efficient method. For a teacher focused on effective whole-class discussion, this might sound like asking questions that encourage students to inquire, or choosing follow-up questions that probe for specificity.

When we understand, we can adjust and apply our learning in varied and unique situations. In complex, real-world circumstances, answers do not come neatly packaged; knowledge and skills are insufficient. When confronted with new challenges and contexts, insight guides effective response. Understanding is evidenced in the doing.

SUPPORTING STUDENT UNDERSTANDING

Understanding gives meaning and coherence to facts and guides their strategic use. As you plan lessons, start with clarity about what students will understand as a result of instruction. Why are you teaching this? You must have an answer beyond, "It's in the standards," "It's in the district curriculum," or "They will need it for 7th grade." You need to be clear about the durable outcomes for students. These big ideas are guideposts to build the lesson around. With your Lesson Study team, ask:

- What counts as learning?
- What essential ideas or principles will stay with students long-term?
- How will students change as a result of instruction?
- What will they comprehend more deeply?

Of course, understanding is always a matter of degree. Through the learning experiences you provide, you move your students along the path toward increased understanding—insight that has value beyond next Friday's test.

Students move along this path to understanding when they have opportunities to apply, analyze, predict, prove, explain, defend, interpret, generalize, synthesize, and make connections. Take one of those verbs and think about how your students will do it in an upcoming lesson.

A benefit of this active approach to learning is that student engagement increases. When work asks students to be curious, thoughtful, and creative, students become absorbed in learning and like it better (Strong, Silver, & Robinson, 1995). Learning activities that foster active intellectual engagement build understanding. Although hands-on activities ensure that students are busy, minds-on activities require cognitive engagement that leads to insight. As you plan, observe, and debrief with your Lesson Study colleagues, you will create a shared vision for what understanding looks and sounds like and have the time to reflect on instructional strategies that facilitate that understanding.

Because understandings are inherently abstract, they cannot be directly taught effectively. This reminds me of a cartoon that shows a picture of a boy standing next to his dog and answering his friend's question. "I said I taught my dog to talk," the boy responds. "I didn't say he learned it." Teaching and learning are related but not synonymous. Learning cannot be thrust upon anyone; they have to open the door for it. For it to count as learning, students need to use what has been taught.

Students learn when they have opportunities to actively construct, compare, collaborate, create, and contribute (Wardlow, 2016). Doing (physically and cognitively) helps students form and reform their ideas and understandings (Kolb, 1984). Doing transforms information into understanding. As you plan lessons with understanding as a goal, think about how students could draw on their cultural knowledge to support their understanding. Think of how you will push at students' conceptions and misconceptions so that their sense-making attempts cause learning.

This is very different from tests that require memorization. Understanding is more than memorizing empty phrases, although memorizing might sometimes be a step in the understanding process. Understanding is more than reading; reading alone does not create understanding, although pondering what was read could lead to it. As you plan your next research lesson, consider the building blocks for understanding. Ask:

- What knowledge and procedures support it?
- What role will doing play in building students' understanding?
- How will students apply concepts to new situations?

Let's consider again the 3rd-grade fractions lesson described in Chapters 5 and 6.

When she taught the lesson, Staci began with an object lesson that illustrated the big ideas of fractions as parts of a whole and of equivalent fractions by placing equal lumps of clay on opposite sides of a balance scale and subsequently dividing and subdividing the lumps. Some students discussed their misunderstanding that a larger quantity would weigh more (i.e., four small lumps vs. two larger lumps). Although understanding might have been deepened had students conducted this experiment for themselves rather than watching the teacher, the visual nevertheless provided a memorable representation to enhance the paper-and-pencil work that followed and to support concept development rather than simply plugging numbers into an algorithm.

It gave meaning to the work. Through the demonstration, 3rd-graders' understanding increased: They were better able to grasp the meaning of fractions; they noted how fractions function; they saw the mathematical problems in relation to other things.

The Lesson Study team that planned and taught this lesson thought about understanding as they designed the learning experience. They watched for understanding as the lesson unfolded. They discussed understanding (and misunderstanding) during the debrief session that followed, and they changed the lesson to better support understanding in subsequent iterations of the lesson.

As you focus on understanding, the observation powers you develop as observers during Lesson Study will transfer to your own classroom. As you teach, you will become less worried about what you are doing as a teacher and more tuned in to student understanding—the ultimate goal of instruction.

DEVELOPING TEACHER UNDERSTANDING

Patterson and Tolnay (2015) suggest that the job of teachers is to be the lead learner. If your goal for students is to increase understanding, it is also a goal for you. There is always more to understand about students, about teaching and learning. Understanding continues to increase as you learn from and with students and colleagues through Lesson Study.

Understanding Others

In its interpersonal meaning, understanding suggests a feeling of rapport. It suggests empathizing with other people and their situations, considering others' points of view. This type of understanding requires us to grasp different ways of being, different styles and purposes for communicating. It is harmony born of respect.

To respect people different from ourselves (and isn't that everyone!), we have to open our minds to ideas that seem unusual and overcome our habitual responses. These attempts help us to understand someone else's understanding.

Understanding Students. Understanding our students is a disciplined attempt to feel as they feel, to see as they see (Wiggins & McTighe, 2005). With understanding comes empathy for other people or cultures. It is to view through their worldview, to walk in their shoes. Understanding builds on positive assumptions, working to find the plausible and meaningful in students' ideas. Even if I can't fully understand, I can recognize and respectfully acknowledge their perspective.

If a student's idea seems murky, I call up what I know about that child. How does his statement relate to our previous learning as a class? To his own prior knowledge and cultural experiences? When I can't see the sense in a student's response, rather than assuming flawed thinking, I can ask, "Why do you think so?" The student's response enhances my understanding. When we take the time to understand students' line of reasoning, to explore how their thinking connects with their personal experiences, our understanding increases.

We develop understanding of our students as we know them and know about them. We empathize with the student who is helping to support the family through an after-school job at a sandwich shop, and we recognize how this experience could contribute to her understanding of the principles of supply and demand in the upcoming economics lesson. This becomes part of the plan for instruction. When planning a 4th-grade literacy lesson with her Lesson Study team, Cindy recognized that her student Phillip, because of difficulty with visual tracking, would have a hard time following along during the read-aloud if the text was projected using the document camera, so she offered printed copies as an option. She didn't single Phillip out, and several others took advantage of this accommodation as well. Cindy's empathy supported Phillip's learning.

To understand students is to consider learning from their perspective. In Lesson Study, we do this during planning, as we think about students' prior knowledge. We do this during our pre-observation meeting, when we anticipate how students will respond. During our debrief, we consider students' perspectives again when we describe what we saw or heard and explain why it matters.

Understanding Colleagues. Lesson Study is enhanced when team members seek to understand one another. If we "seek first to understand, then to be understood" (Covey, 2004, p. 235), we gain perspective and insight. When we fully consider the ideas of others, we may come to recognize our own assumptions, our own subjectivity. As we reveal our ideas to colleagues, who listen with the same respect, mutual understanding develops.

Working through the Lesson Study process with colleagues, we will find similarities in our thinking, and we will find differences. We don't have to reconcile differences, just recognize and respectfully acknowledge them.

Our respect causes us to be open-minded, to carefully consider colleagues' views even when they are different from our own. Perhaps especially when they are different from our own, because it is then that they really have something to teach us. We are allied with our colleagues, and it is a productive alliance, because they will see things that we don't. Hearing our colleagues' perspectives can cause us to rethink a situation.

Understanding Teaching and Learning

Through Lesson Study, knowledge about instruction is embodied in people and systems, not only in the artifacts, such as lesson plans, that are created.

Understanding resides in the minds of those who create it for themselves. This individual and collective wisdom infuses teachers' enactment of instruction over time and across contexts.

Pedagogical Knowledge. When we understand instruction, global generalizations about teaching and learning have meaning for us. Truisms such as "Connecting new ideas to background knowledge increases learning" and "Talking can be rehearsal for writing" conjure examples from our experience, specifics that give meaning to the expression.

Lesson Study supports specific insights, building procedural understandings about the art and science of teaching. For example, Bethani demonstrated understanding during the debrief of the 1st-grade geometry Lesson Study at Old Wire Elementary described in Chapter 4. She suggested that inserting an opportunity for partner talk would increase engagement during a long stretch of whole-group discussion, showing her understanding of pacing. Similarly, Cheri demonstrated understanding when, following a 4th-grade literacy lesson, she suggested that using an onscreen timer during small-group work would keep students focused.

Disciplinary Knowledge. In 1986, Lee Shulman described the disciplinary knowledge that is important for teachers. The concept of pedagogical content knowledge, as Shulman labeled it, has had sticking power because it encompasses understandings that teachers need to have to teach a discipline effectively. Such understanding goes beyond knowledge of facts and concepts of the discipline, including useful forms for representing those ideas that make them comprehensible to others. What demonstrations, examples, and illustrations are helpful? What experiences guide students to these concepts? Knowing the content is not enough—teachers must also know how to convey those ideas to others.

In addition, teachers benefit from understanding the structure of the discipline. What are the big ideas? How are they related? In what ways have these ideas been organized to support their comprehensibility? For example, historians might think about the key concepts of significance, continuity and change, cause and effect, and perspective to support understanding of historical events and issues. Using overarching concepts to guide instruction is an example of disciplinary knowledge.

Intellectual Gratification. Working with colleagues through Lesson Study, you can ask questions such as those above to enhance your disciplinary knowledge. Planning together and discussing lessons will also increase your pedagogical knowledge. Although both have been labeled as knowledge, I hope you will have understanding as your goal, because the intellectual gratification that comes from struggle and eventual insight is invigorating! We find pleasure in the "life of the mind" as we satisfy our curiosity (Keene, 2008, p. 6). Your understanding will develop as you build on your existing knowledge, consider your context and your students' cultures, and explore together your perceptions, assumptions, beliefs, and interpretations.

Understanding gives you flexibility to remember, reuse, revise, and reapply ideas (Keene, 2008). Your experiences become points of reference that help you get your bearings when new situations arise. Extracting the underlying principles from your teaching experiences helps you show grace under pressure and solve new problems (Bransford, Brown, & Cocking, 2000; Wiggins & McTighe, 2005). In a world where information and knowledge are ubiquitously available, the understanding you have gained will serve you as you make both planned and spontaneous instructional decisions.

Reflect and Respond

---

1. ***Read*** and annotate the following quote:

> In Bernard Pomerance's (1977) play *The Elephant Man*, the deformed main character, Merrick, has the experience of being listened to for the first time—and he finds he can speak: "Before I spoke with people, I did not think of those things because there was no one to think them for. But now things come out of my mouth that are true."
> —in Newkirk, 2017, p. 78

Reflect & Respond: Think of a time when talking with others increased your understanding. How was talking helpful?

2. ***Read or watch*** one of the following:

   - https://www.teachingchannel.org/blog/2016/01/22/5-tips-conceptual-understanding
   - http://www.evidencebasedteaching.org.au/deep-understanding/
   - https://tinyurl.com/Ch7-Understand

Reflect & Respond:

   - From whichever item above you reviewed, what insights did you gain about developing students' understanding?

3. ***Read*** the following quote:

> The growth of understanding follows an ascending spiral rather than a straight line.
> —Joanna Field, 1934, as quoted in Maggio, 1992, p. 331

Reflect & Respond: Put the quote above into your own words and illustrate it with something you have learned about.

Self-Assess: In this chapter, you read about how to develop students' understanding by giving them opportunities to apply, analyze, predict, prove, explain, defend, interpret, generalize, synthesize, and make connections. Which of these could you include more of in an upcoming lesson?

CHAPTER 8

Flexibility

Understanding enables flexibility. Great bakers understand how to adjust ingredients based on their knowledge of how those ingredients interact. A baker knows how to adjust the liquid in a cake recipe on a humid day, how to adjust the baking powder at higher altitudes, how to balance sweetness with spice. Similarly, exemplary teachers know how to adjust a lesson when students are energetic or talkative, when they are confused, or when they are ready to be challenged. Knowing the active ingredients in a lesson, those most important experiences that will enable learning, allows flexibility with other aspects of the lesson.

In this chapter, we'll examine how to be flexible within your carefully planned lesson, and how such flexibility is considered within the Lesson Study cycle.

TEACHING REQUIRES COGNITIVE FLEXIBILITY

Teaching can be enormously rewarding and enormously challenging. It is an activity that calls upon all of our mental faculties, an enormous intellectual experience. If you are a high school teacher, you may find your content mentally engaging; a kindergarten teacher may not be challenged by the simple mathematical knowledge his students are acquiring, but the pedagogical knowledge and pedagogical content knowledge necessary for optimal learning are immense. Teaching is a complex, contextualized activity requiring multifactor decisionmaking. Planning an effective lesson requires understanding; adjusting that plan appropriately as the lesson unfolds requires insight and cognitive flexibility (Spiro & Jehng, 1990).

During Lesson Study, you work hard with your team to plan a lesson that is based on best practices, guided by research and your own experiences. You can identify the active ingredients in the lesson, those key pieces that make it work. These are the lesson's core elements, things you want to stay true to. The word *fidelity* has negative connotations of rigidity and scriptedness, which should be avoided. Instead, you want to have fidelity to the core elements of a lesson while adjusting to your students' needs. Research suggests best practices, but there appears to be a point of diminishing return for fidelity (Harn,

Parisi, & Stoolmiller, 2013). Flexibility, not unshakeable fidelity, is central to effective instruction (Chun & Dickson, 2011; Higgins & Parsons, 2009; Prater & Devereaux, 2009; Smit & van Eerde, 2013). Students benefit when the active ingredients of a lesson are maintained, but they are not well served when a detailed plan is followed in spite of, rather than because of, the way learning unfolds.

Students are constantly giving the teacher information to guide the remainder of the lesson. Instruction is a dance. You must be on your toes, nimble, ready to follow a student's lead. You have to think on your feet. You can skip steps when there's evidence that students have already mastered them, adding a more complex turn. Or you can slow the pace to allow for needed practice or explanation.

There will always be some tension between the desire to manage a lesson efficiently and the desire to be flexible based on students' interests and needs. Anticipating students' responses, as you do with your team before teaching and observing a research lesson, prepares you to stay balanced as the lesson unfolds, keeping your learning targets in view as you adjust to students' needs. Because no two classes are the same, materials, methods, and pacing will differ. Flexibility acknowledges the variability of your students.

Flexibility with the Lesson Plan

As you planned the research lesson with colleagues, you selected materials and methods that were congruent with evidence-based best practices and aligned with your students' interests, needs, and experiences. When you planned, you may have started with your school's curricular resources, or you may have built the lesson from scratch. Either way, you thought about your students and your purposes as you constructed the lesson. You didn't just include something in the lesson because a teachers' guide said to. You used these resources flexibly to match your students. Flexibility began during the planning phase as you created your plan and decided what materials to use.

Then, during the pre-observation meeting, you predicted students' responses to each part of the lesson and anticipated how the teacher could respond. Maybe you tightened up parts of the lesson based on this conversation. Going into the research lesson, the teacher has a solid plan. Because of this thoughtful preparation, the teacher is well positioned to be flexible when teaching based on what she sees and hears from students. As the lesson plays out, there will be opportunities for flexibility. Take them.

Deviations from the plan might include changing materials or adjusting instructional methods. When the teacher chooses to deviate from what was planned based on students' responses, she is choosing to be flexible with the plan—to make adjustments, even though her team had different ideas going into the lesson. Such adjustments are made in the best interest of students.

Several times, during a Lesson Study debrief, I've heard the teacher who was being observed say something like, "I knew it wasn't working, but I thought

I needed to stick with our plan," or, "Ordinarily, I would have changed this, but since you were watching . . . " These assumptions, unfortunately, denied observers an opportunity to see how adjustments might have improved the lesson. And, more important, students were denied the opportunity for richer learning that might have occurred had the adjustments been made. You are not tied to your plan. Even during research lesson observations—especially during research lesson observations—students always come first. Observers will learn more from seeing how the adjustments play out than from watching a less effective lesson.

So, if a read-aloud book is too far outside kids' experiences, stop reading it. If the number line isn't working as a visual for fractions, pull out the Unifix Cubes. I'm not suggesting willy-nilly changes or premature abandonment of a text or manipulative. But if the evidence you are collecting—from students' faces, comments, or work—suggests the need for a change, make it. If staying the course means you will never reach your destination, it's time for a change. Be prepared to move with the minds of your classroom.

If the instructional strategy you had planned is not leading to learning, modify or abandon it, even if you are being observed. If a class arrives chatty and energetic, add an opening activity that involves talking and movement, using their powers for good! If group-work is leading to confusion, pull the whole class back together. If students aren't engaged with the video, read-aloud, or presentation, stop it and have a discussion. Because you understand the learning goals for the lesson, you will recognize when a change in materials or methods is needed to get you there.

Flexibility Within the Lesson Plan

Sometimes changes to the lesson plan are needed so that goals can be achieved. Often, however, your lesson plays out pretty much as expected. Even then, flexibility is perceptible, if observers have eyes to see it, if reflective practitioners make note of it. Flexibility within the plan means that the lesson meanders a bit along its intended course, but the route stays the same. There is space for flexibility between the lines of the lesson plan.

One area of subtle flexibility is the lesson's pacing. If students are lethargic, you pick up the pace yourself and see if they come with you. If some students are perplexed, you slow down, perhaps returning to the point of confusion and revisiting content. As you reflect on the lesson, ask: Which parts of the lesson were moved through more quickly? Where did the lesson linger, and why? These are things to make note of as the lesson moves forward and to discuss later when you debrief. Talking it through will make you more cognizant of and deliberate about such decisions in the future.

Another aspect of the lesson where flexibility is evident is during discussions between teacher and student. These include whole-class conversations, time working with small groups, and individual conferences. Sometimes, in these situations, a student's response is what was expected, and no adjustment is necessary. When we know our students well, we make generally good predictions about the course of a conversation. But the details will always surprise us, and sometimes conversations take an unexpected turn. The ability to respond spontaneously is important and is built on understanding of students, content, and pedagogy. It is honed by experience.

Teachers demonstrate lack of flexibility when they ignore a student's comment or genuine question or when they quickly dismiss it. Learning is supported when, instead, a teacher listens and asks questions to better understand students' reasoning or to clarify or extend students' thinking. Seeing the potential of an idea, the teacher helps students develop it. Productive dialogue occurs when a discussion focuses on important ideas and promotes students' active, personal construction of knowledge (Leikin & Dinur, 2007).

Of course, not every student comment leads in this direction. If a student's question or comment sidesteps the conversation in an unproductive way (deliberately or unintentionally), a respectful response maintains the inquisitive culture of the classroom while effectively moving learning forward. Effectiveness requires a sensible balance between flexibility and firmness. If you are observing, note how the teacher uses her judgment in discussion decisions, staying with or respectfully deferring a response. How is the delicate balance of pacing and responsiveness maintained? A teacher's understanding helps her respond appropriately to student comments. Flexibility like this doesn't change the lesson plan, which has been painted in fairly broad strokes. Flexibility within the plan comes in the fine-grained details.

FLEXIBILITY VS. THE PERFECT LESSON PLAN

Every classroom has a different combination of learners who have unique needs and experiences. Every classroom also has its unique collective culture: webs of relationships, ways of doing and caring, and shared experiences. Because of this variation, there are many, many aspects of a lesson that require a flexible response. Understanding your goals and the active ingredients of your lesson helps you know where to stay firm and where to be flexible with your plan for a lesson.

Re*Visioning* through Lesson Study is not about creating the perfect lesson plan; it is about understanding the active ingredients, those best practices that can be applied to or lifted from a lesson. After a lesson has been taught, you re*Vision* it, conceiving and developing a version that seems right for you and your students. Over time and across lessons, strategies will emerge that represent best practices. And, as Allan Luke (2016) suggested, "When practices are embodied by teachers, they don't go away."

You will teach in more sophisticated ways as you know what you have committed to and why, as you are responsive to what is going on in the classroom but are headed all the while toward your goals, meandering as needed along the route.

Abby Neighbors, an intern at Old Wire Elementary, was developing this understanding. When teaching a math lesson on comparing fractions, she recognized early on that her students seemed confused by her explanation about comparing fractions with the same denominator. Even though a lot of time had gone into planning the lesson with her team, and she had mentally rehearsed it over and over, she knew she shouldn't plow ahead when students seemed perplexed. Backing up, she showed a short video that illustrated the idea, giving visual examples that compared fractions like 1/4, 2/4, and 3/4, so that students understood the concept of what the numerator and denominator meant. Then, with students' increased insight, the lesson moved forward as planned. Abby was demonstrating flexibility.

A closed lesson, one that is followed with exactness, will likely have stratified results, with some students left confused. If, instead, instruction is flexible and responsive, students have a more level playing field and increased opportunities for success.

Instruction and learning are complex, contextualized activities, so it isn't possible to have a prepackaged description of how to respond in every situation (Collet, 2011). Teachers must have the cognitive flexibility to opportunistically use instructional strategies (Spiro, Collins, & Ramchandran, 2007). There will never be a perfect lesson plan. Teaching is improvable, but not perfectible, because classrooms and schools are complex contexts that require flexibility.

FLEXIBILITY AS A FOCUS FOR LESSON STUDY

Experience with Lesson Study can help you be more sensitive to the learning context and more aware of alternatives. Recognizing an appropriate degree of flexibility is a sign of expert, effective instruction.

Unfortunately, pressures of accountability policies may create rigid responses to curriculum, where top-down decisionmaking restricts flexibility and inhibits teachers' use of their knowledge and understanding; such a response actually reduces the system's ability to meet demands (Butler & Schnellert, 2012; Ciminelli et al., 2009; Daly, 2009; Rosenblatt, 2004; Staw, Sandelands, & Dutton, 1981). That's what initially happened at Parker Elementary when it was marked as a Turnaround school. Teachers like Allie, Linda, and Kim felt restrained and disempowered. This type of pressure creates an overemphasis on testing, constrains the curriculum, limits teacher flexibility, and reduces classroom quality (Plank & Condliffe, 2013). Fortunately, through their participation in the Lesson Study cycle, teachers at Parker regained their instructional agency.

Study

Each phase of the Lesson Study cycle encourages teachers' agency. As the 5th-grade teachers at Parker set out to design lessons specific to their students' needs, they reviewed research and considered a variety of curricular resources. During the study phase of the Lesson Study cycle, Allie, Linda, and Kim pulled from their shelves books by Calkins (2013), Auman (2003), and Mariconda and Aurey (2005). They looked at their district's language arts curriculum and learned from the strategies and activities that were recommended. They read articles describing evidence-based best practices. They also talked about their own past experiences and analyzed data from their school and their own students.

The study phase of the cycle was filled with inquiry and dialogue, sharing and the bandying of ideas. Members of the team would suggest, examine, advocate, reason, and persuade. Studying research, resources, and data prepared them for flexibility as they planned.

Plan

Like the teachers at Parker, you have many ideas to consider when planning a lesson, giving you the opportunity to reflect and select learning experiences that are well suited for your students. Rather than sticking rigidly to a predetermined curriculum, during Lesson Study, your team flexibly designs learning experiences that target both the lesson objectives and your students' specific needs.

To refine the lesson, you consider how students might respond to these activities and even chart out teachers' responses, constructing hypothetical learning trajectories and searching for different solutions. Anticipating these scenarios prepares you to react in ways that support students' learning. Experience and careful observation make your predictions more accurate.

Observe

During the observation phase of Lesson Study, you become more acutely aware of teachable moments when segments of the instruction seem to flow, when students are engaged and inquiring. The colleague who is teaching is observing, too, and will sense and seize these moments in the lesson and make the most of them, digging deeper with questions, encouraging students to explore ideas with one another, perhaps moving away from the planned trajectory to seize an opportunity. This is reflection-in-action (Schön, 1987) or flexibility-in-action (Leikin & Dinur, 2007). Those observing will take notes, preparing for later analysis.

Powerful teaching requires paying close attention to how things are going and then acting accordingly. This principle applies when students are struggling as well as excelling. Whether it is one student or many who are not moving along in the learning journey, flexibility with the planned path improves outcomes. Being conscientiously consistent with key ingredients and frequently flexible when the situation provokes it increases student learning.

Reflect

Considering flexibility during reflection, you and your team can ask, "How was this different from what we had in mind?" During this phase of the Lesson Study cycle, the enacted lesson is compared with what was planned and anticipated.

Analyzing the instantiation of your plan in light of your expectations bridges the gap from facts you have collected to understanding principles of learning. Through reflection, you can become more capable of flexibility-in-action during future instruction and more creative and effective when planning.

Re*Vision*

Reflection supports re*Visioning* of instruction. Much like the initial planning phase, re*Visioning* is informed and guided by your goals and your students' needs, and having seen the lesson enacted, you have a clearer understanding of both. Your experiences inform your professional decisionmaking.

Using a debrief chart (refer to Figure 6.3), your team captures what you noticed during observation and why it is important. You analyze the experiences and the outcomes. These insights help you determine what to hang onto and what to adjust or set aside in future iterations of the lesson. They enable flexible preparation rather than strict adherence to a preset curriculum.

Reteach

Reteaching provides another iteration of the observe-reflect-re*Vision* cycle, applying the learning in your own classroom. You might opportunistically build on your own students' interests and knowledge, perhaps using a basketball example when an enthusiast of the game struggles with the concept of averages, pulling statistics from a current hero to illustrate. Knowledge of the lesson couples with knowledge of your students, creating significant learning opportunities.

Lesson Study can make you more cognizant of your own flexibility. It's exciting to notice your aptitude for improvisation growing. Experience makes you more adept at calling up alternative approaches for solving problems; your instructional repertoire increases.

INCREASED FLEXIBILITY

Participation in the Lesson Study process increases flexibility. Those new to Lesson Study tend to write precise, detailed lesson directions, whereas experienced participants plan lessons by drawing a map that offers multiple pathways to the destination (Takahashi, Watanabe, Yoshida, & Wang-Iverson, 2005). Their understanding allows them to envision alternate routes.

Teaching is a profession that requires perpetual change (Garcia & O'Donnell-Allen, 2015). Perfected lessons are not the goal of Lesson Study; rather, the goal is ongoing professional growth (Lewis & Hurd, 2011). Teachers improve the lesson "as a way to deepen their own content knowledge, their knowledge of student thinking, their understanding of teaching, and their commitment to improvement of their own practice and that of colleagues" (p. 24). Lesson Study is not about discovering the one right way to teach a lesson, but about building teacher understanding.

Experience leads to understanding. Understanding and flexibility are companion principles that we should strive to apply concurrently and consistently. We act in the present while simultaneously looking to the past for direction. Effective flexibility is inextricably tied to understanding of content, pedagogy, and students. This trifecta of insight grows through participation in the Lesson Study cycle. Lesson Study supports teachers in their own ongoing learning journey.

Reflect and Respond

---

1. ***Read*** and annotate the following quote:

   > Ensuring learning requires paying close attention to how things are going and being prepared to act accordingly. This applies also when it is just one student, or a few students, who are struggling. An experienced and conscientious teacher will find a way to ensure that all students learn.
   >
   > —Danielson, 2011, p. 90

   Reflect & Respond: Why is flexibility necessary to ensure learning?

2. ***Read or watch*** one of the following:
   - https://tinyurl.com/Ch8-Flexible-Teacher
   - https://tinyurl.com/Ch8-Be-Flexible
   - https://www.teacher.org/daily/demonstrating-flexibility-responsiveness-classroom/

   Reflect & Respond:
   - What new ideas about being flexible did you get from the item you selected above?

3. **Read** the following quote:

> That which yields is not always weak.
>
> —Jacqueline Carey, 2001, p. 222

Reflect & Respond: How does this simple phrase relate to teaching and flexibility?

Self-Assess: Consider a lesson you recently taught. How was it different from what you had planned? Did the flexibility enhance or inhibit students' learning?

Supporting Responsiveness

In the preceding chapters, we considered understanding and flexibility as goals for Lesson Study. Building on these concepts, Chapter 9 adds the notion of responsiveness. Understanding, flexibility, and responsiveness influence one another in an ongoing process. This helix is like a coil, and as it spirals upward it expands and widens. Understanding, flexibility, and responsiveness are not separate and discrete; rather, they are intertwined and continuous. The understanding that both fuels and is fed by this ongoing process develops, evolves, and changes with experience and attention.

In an era where teachers are sometimes treated as deskilled technicians, Lesson Study emphasizes the thinking role of teachers as they hone their professional craft and continually adjust instruction to align with students' cultures, interests, and needs. As teachers consider and build upon the background knowledge and skills each learner brings to the social context of the classroom, learning increases. Teacher judgment and responsiveness are at the center of curricular decisions.

Responsiveness occurs during planning, as teachers analyze students' work and adapt upcoming activities, designing scaffolding that is tailored to students' needs or including activities that draw on students' funds of knowledge (Moll et al., 2006). Responsiveness occurs during instruction, when in-the-moment decisions simultaneously account for students' cultures, interests, and needs. Responsiveness means seizing an opportunity to enhance learning, perhaps building on a spontaneous event; it means persistently scaffolding a student who needs help, drawing on a repertoire of strategies.

Responsiveness takes generalized best practices that have been economically stripped to their essentials and brings them to life, embodying them with ambiance and detail, making them a memorable part of teachers' lived experiences. Specific contexts, thoughts, and feelings exemplify abstract principles. The practical and the theoretical are married as best practices become "both a source for specific ideas and a heuristic to stimulate new thinking" (Shulman, 1986, p. 12). Through teachers' examination of specific cases where research-based practices have been implemented, Lesson Study makes best practices part of the institutional memory of the school, ready for future use.

CULTURAL RESPONSIVENESS

Educational theories and practices must always be reinvented and adapted to the worlds and lived experiences of the learners. Teachers choose activities and materials that help them recruit their students' knowledge in order to meet learning objectives (Hassett, 2008). Cultural identities, practices, and tools that students possess become a rich resource for learning. As you design instruction that builds on these resources, your instruction becomes more culturally responsive.

Ways of Doing

Culturally responsive instruction is a manifestation of appreciation of different ways of knowing and doing (Howard & Rodriguez-Minkoff, 2017). Culturally responsive teachers adjust their teaching to the background of their students, instead of requiring the opposite. Too often, schools have adopted White, middle-class norms, expecting students of all backgrounds to leave their own identities at the door. So many opportunities are lost when this happens! Students' own cultural resources, their experiences and ways of thinking and responding, can be harnessed for learning when teachers allow (and even encourage) it. I loved the experience I had with Lesson Study at Stilwell High School, which demonstrates this so well.

As explained in Chapter 3, Stilwell High School has a high percentage of Native American students. One of the Lesson Study teams at Stilwell High includes Charity, who is White and has taught at Stilwell High for over 20 years, and her colleagues, Tasha and Lisa, who both have some Native American ancestry. Lisa is married to a very traditional Cherokee. She also has a degree in Native American Studies.

The research lesson we designed was about how punctuation supports meaning in writing. During the lesson, which was taught by Tasha, students worked in groups of three to puzzle together sentence strips and form a cohesive paragraph. In our debrief, we discussed one group in depth. Charity had noticed that "no matter what [Tasha] did, they just **did not** talk." Charity asked, "Is this cultural?" Because there had been minimal vocalization, she wondered if these students were learning.

Two of the three students in the group were being raised in traditional Cherokee homes and used high-context communication (Ageyev, 2003); gestures and situational cues were important to understanding. There was not much talking while they worked on the collaborative tasks.

Lisa pointed out that these two students had communicated mostly with eye movements and slight gestures (as noted in Figure 9.1). We checked their papers and noticed that they had ended up with similar responses, even though they hadn't said much. The students' shared traditional communication methods were an asset to their collaboration. The third member of their group, who was not Native American, was less successful. He didn't pick up on subtle cues of how the other two group members were thinking.

During the debrief, we unpacked what had happened, discussed grouping alternatives, and eventually determined that at times it was helpful to group Cherokee students together so they could work in ways that used their cultural tools. Our conversation increased our awareness of students' cultural resources.

Looking closely at individual learning can lead to additional differentiation of lessons and new understandings about how culture influences instruction. As you work to make your lessons more responsive, you will become aware of the variation within your own classroom, which will spur ideas for how to take advantage of your students' unique cultural resources.

As noted earlier, in the United States, over 80% of teachers are White, middle-class, and monolingual (U.S. Department of Education, 2016). In contrast, 51% of K–12 students were nonwhite in the 2015–2016 school year. So most teachers in today's schools, although well intentioned, may be quite unaware of the cultural knowledge and practices that their students bring from their homes and communities. At Stilwell, we were fortunate that Lisa brought

Figure 9.1. Stilwell Debrief Chart Excerpt

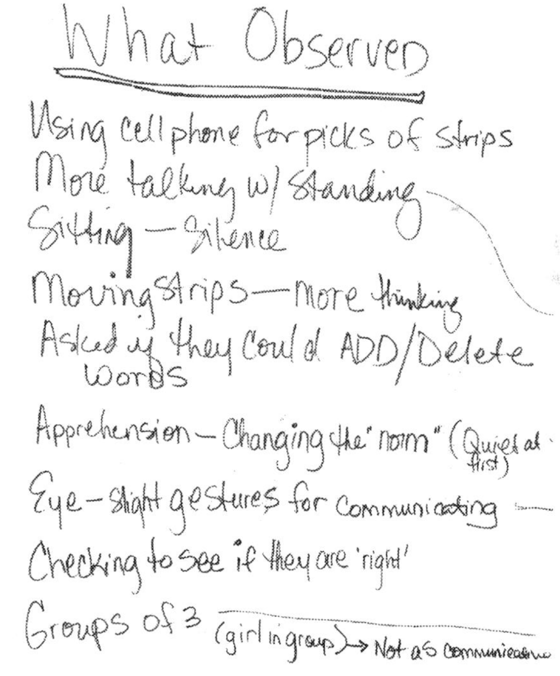

What Observed

Using cell phone for picks of strips
More talking w/ standing
Sitting — silence
Moving strips — more thinking
Asked if they could ADD/Delete words
Apprehension — Changing the "norm" (Quiet at first)
Eye — slight gestures for communicating
Checking to see if they are 'right'
Groups of 3 (girl in group) → Not as communicative

an insider's perspective. But with so many different cultures represented in today's diverse classrooms, it's hard to know the cultural resources our students possess. How can teachers overcome this cultural knowledge gap?

Research is an important part of the study phase of the Lesson Study cycle. If a goal is to improve the cultural responsiveness of your teaching, your team will want to investigate assets of the cultures represented in your classrooms. Of course, book learning provides only general information about cultural ways of knowing and doing. Paying close attention to your own students will give you clues about whether your students' skills, dispositions, and knowledge align with what you've read. At Stilwell, even though most of the students had some Native American ancestry, fewer were being raised in traditional ways and exhibited Cherokee ways of doing. Watching students closely revealed these traits. Talking with students and their families can also uncover their cultural knowledge.

Funds of Knowledge

Students' lived experiences give them knowledge that can be a bridge to school learning. Culturally responsive teaching connects academic abstractions to the cultural and cognitive resources of students' homes and cultures. The knowledge and skills that keep a home humming and pass along cultural conventions can and should influence how we do school. Learning is supported when we connect the new to the known.

At Old Wire Elementary School, where about 65% of the population is Latinx, it makes sense to use the book *Too Many Tamales* (Soto & Martinez, 1996) to teach about making predictions. Although teaching about other cultures is important, it's critical that students, especially students from historically marginalized populations, see themselves and their own experiences in the school's curriculum.

Family experiences also provide a resource for learning. At Old Wire, many of the students have parents or relatives who work construction jobs. Word problems asking students to use a math strategy to decide how many two-by-fours are needed for a wall make the work meaningful and use students' home experiences as a resource. Connecting instructional concepts with students' personal experiences and cultural resources supports their learning.

Language

Language is a cultural instrument and a resource for learning. Responsive teachers view bilingualism as an additive resource students bring to the classroom. Language shapes thought, so having more than one language gives thought more shape! When a student explains an idea to his peer in a second language that they share, he thinks about the concept in another way and deepens the learning for them both. What an asset!

If we strategically position partners or let students choose their own, we can support English learners by including think-pair-share and letting students choose the language they'll use when they talk to their partner. This gives them a chance to rehearse an idea in their native tongue before bringing it to the group.

When teachers value and privilege the benefits of bilingualism, learning is enhanced. By being attuned to students' language resources, you can find ways of connecting students' everyday language practices with academic language and literacy skills, and your instruction becomes more responsive.

Culturally Responsive Dispositions

Teachers legitimize students' cultural ways of knowing and doing by bringing them into the classroom. Recognizing opportunities for these connections, both planned and spontaneous, makes your instruction more responsive. When you look for these opportunities, you are making students contributors to and agents of their own learning (Lizárraga & Gutiérrez, 2018).

You develop and demonstrate culturally responsive dispositions when you seek and use students' cultural gifts and knowledge in their school learning. Students of all backgrounds have a wealth of cultural knowledge that you can tap into. When students are encouraged to use their cultural toolkit, they engage more fully and their learning increases.

CONTEXTUAL RESPONSIVENESS

Your community and classroom context are also learning resources. Contextually appropriate practice increases learning. During Lesson Study, developing local lessons allows for content to be contextually responsive. Community knowledge is a resource that you and your colleagues consider as you plan research lessons that are responsive to local issues and problems. You map effective practices onto the research lesson in ways that are contextualized for your students.

Contextually responsive teaching is an antidote to step-by-step, one-size-fits-all programs. Effective teaching is a two-way street, both specific and generalizable. Best practices inform and are informed by context. Effective teaching requires attention to generalized ideas about best practices and to the specific context of your learners. The lessons you create are specific to the contexts of your communities and classrooms, but the knowledge you gain is generalizable.

Community Context

In Berryville, a rural Arkansas community that uses Lesson Study at all grade levels, life is tied to the rhythm of the seasons, to planting and harvesting, to calving and milking. Although many students live in town and don't experience these things firsthand, it is community knowledge that impacts life in their small town. A math problem dealing with temperature change draws on students' contextual knowledge. A problem about a parking garage does not.

One of the Lesson Study teams learned this during a middle school math lesson. Working in small groups, students rotated through stations with different story problems. They created words, tables, equations, and graphs to represent linear equations. At the station with a problem about cell phones, students jumped right in; they had extensive knowledge about cell phones and the need for proximity to the cell tower in their community. The problem about fees at a parking garage seemed more confusing to students, however. As we discussed this during debrief, we realized there wasn't a parking garage within 50 miles of Berryville!

Similarly, a 5th-grade literacy lesson at Berryville that was focused on making inferences fell short because it was based on a read-aloud of *The Latke Who Couldn't Stop Screaming* (Snicket, 2007). Students seemed confused by the content and weren't able to notice "aha" moments like we'd hoped. We realized students had had little exposure to Jewish culture. There is no synagogue in Berryville or surrounding communities, so understanding the references to Jewish traditions would have required extensive preteaching.

Lessons that are socially situated in students' lives draw on their knowledge as a resource for learning and can be applied beyond the task at hand. Discussions and thinking are richer and application more probable when skills and content are tied to community knowledge.

A Wealth of Experiences

All students have life experiences that can be connected to school learning. Teachers sometimes view families with limited economic resources as also being poor in terms of the quality of experiences they provide for their child. That is only true if we are blind to the connections between the curriculum and students' personal experiences.

Children in low-income families learn collaboration through working and playing together. They learn creativity by finding a new use for old objects. They learn the value of things by working or waiting for them. Maybe knowing how to read the bus schedule will help them with those elapsed-time problems in math class. Maybe their experiences at the laundromat taught them how many quarters make two dollars. We don't wish poverty on anyone, but we can see all students' experiences as additive, not subtractive. We can build on the experiences students bring to classrooms, seeing the interconnectedness of the multiple sites of learning that children navigate (Lizárraga & Gutiérrez, 2018). Compassion shouldn't become pious pity that minimizes what children have to offer.

Children often recognize the richness of their own experiences. I was surprised when a student teacher talked about how sorry she felt for the child in her class who had to share a bed with a sibling. The student teacher thought this must be a hardship for the child, diminishing her privacy and her sleep. I thought back on my own childhood, when I had shared a double bed in the basement with my sister. For years, we followed a familiar routine every night of chatting with each other before we drifted off to sleep. While the student teacher felt sorry for the child in her class, I couldn't imagine why my happy memories might be considered a privation. One person's rags are another's riches! Responsive teachers mine all students' experiences for meaningful connections to in-school learning rather than viewing some students' experiences through a deficit lens.

What gems from students' background knowledge can you connect to the curriculum? Your students will see the richness of their own experiences as you draw upon them as classroom resources. Instruction that connects to students' social worlds and the resources of the community is rich and multidimensional.

Classroom Context

The context of your own classroom is also a resource for learning, a way to be responsive to your students' experiences. Throughout the year, your students have had experiences together that you can draw on to support current objectives. Such connectedness brings cohesion to learning, a wholeness that makes school meaningful. These are adaptations you make to the research lesson when teaching it in your own classroom.

> When Ms. Smith read *The Story of Ruby Bridges* (Coles & Ford, 2010) to her 2nd-grade students, she asked them to think about the character traits that Ruby demonstrated. During their discussion of the book, students spontaneously made connections to the character Molly in the book *Stand Tall, Molly Lou Melon* (Lovell & Catrow, 2011), which they'd read earlier. They discussed how both characters demonstrated courage and confidence. Although Molly Lou is a fictional character, the discussion of character traits when reading this story became a resource for building historical empathy with Ruby Bridges. The connection made between these two experiences is an example of instruction that is responsive to classroom context.

Whenever you say, "Remember last week, when we . . ." or "We'll use this tomorrow to . . . ," you are building on your classroom context.

Mr. Perry was doing this kind of building during a kindergarten lesson on plants as food when he reminded students about the lettuce they fed their class pet, a rabbit they had named Snowball (ironically, Snowball was a black rabbit!). Ms. Sanchez was doing this kind of building in her high school anatomy class when she reminded students that their classmate, Jack, had broken his tibia in a recent football game. Learning that is responsive to the context of your classroom will be more meaningful and memorable.

Each classroom is a context characterized by specific knowledge, perspectives, values, relationships, and norms. Over time, students develop ways of engaging with this community. Responsive teachers look for opportunities to actively build and then draw upon these characteristics. Such opportunities will be both planned for and spontaneous. Watch for them throughout the Lesson Study cycle.

Responsive teachers have the same lesson manuals that everyone else has, but they use them as resources to plan and enact instruction that reflects community and classroom contexts. They know each class has a different collective memory to draw from. They know the present moment offers opportunities they can't anticipate, and they are willing to respond.

RESPONSIVENESS TO INDIVIDUAL LIVES AND INTERESTS

Responsive teaching means building on students' contexts and cultures. An understanding of these group resources can enhance instruction. But beyond group membership, students have individual interests and needs. When teachers know these, they can get personal.

Outside of school, learning is motivated by individual interests and questions. When a similar purpose isn't part of in-school learning, it runs the risk of becoming rote and meaningless beyond the immediate task. Teachers' knowledge of students' lives and interests gives students a reason to engage. When teachers know their students well enough to attach skills to interests, when learning is situated within students' lives, it feels relevant, and lively discussions and deeper thinking ensue. Such instruction connects students' lives to their academic interests, and learning increases.

Students' interests are implicit in and necessary for responsive teaching. Individual responsiveness creates a classroom where students' ideas and opinions are valued.

We gain knowledge of individual students' interests by listening carefully. Getting-to-know-you surveys (like the one in Appendix F) collected at the beginning of the year or semester are a starting place. Greetings at the door as students enter provide an ongoing opportunity for building relationships and gathering information. Find a system to physically or mentally file this information so that it will be ready when you need it during Lesson Study planning or re*Visioning* sessions and in the midst of instruction.

Planned Responsiveness

When teachers know about their students' lives and interests, they can take advantage of this knowledge during lesson planning.

Chapter 4 describes a 1st-grade Lesson Study planning session at Old Wire Elementary School. Preservice teachers Avery, Bethani, and Sarah discussed what they would use to activate students' schema at the beginning of their geometry lesson. Bethani mentioned that she had a couple of kids who wanted to be construction workers like their parents; that could be a connection. She also had a few who wanted to be artists. Avery chimed in that she had also thought about relating the lesson to art, since quite a few students in her class had that interest. So they searched online and found modern art images that had regular geometric shapes. They decided on an image they felt would be perfect for getting students talking about the attributes of shapes. When Avery taught the research lesson, it was clear that students were excited when the bright image appeared on the Smart Board, and they loved coming up to point out the shapes in the art!

This lesson built on students' interests and provided a segue to the academic content. Knowing about class members' interests and lives allows for thoughtful plans that increase engagement. (Note: The plan for this lesson is available in Appendix E.)

Spontaneous Responsiveness

When meaning is negotiated through students' individual interests and identities, learning feels real; it is real. Teachers can gather and instantaneously use information about students' distinct opinions, interests, and experiences in the midst of teaching. This gives the content and skills a relevant purpose.

Ms. Valdez did this while conferring during writers' workshop. Students had selected their own writing topic, and Stephan's was deeply personal: He was writing about his mother's recent trip to Mexico for brain cancer treatments. The class mini-lesson had been on creating visual images, so as Ms. Valdez knelt beside Stephan, she gently probed about an image he would like to convey to the reader. She listened while Stephan whispered about both his loneliness and his mother's pain. Ms. Valdez's sensitivity helped Stephan find the level of risk he felt comfortable taking. Stephan's writing served personal, as well as academic, purposes. This was a private moment that did not become part of a Lesson Study conversation, but Ms. Valdez mentally filed the insight she had gained.

As you find connections between your students' lives and the knowledge and skills you are required to teach, students will feel the potential of their learning. Your responsiveness to students' lives and interests will give them the chance to scrutinize their experiences through a larger lens.

RESPONSIVENESS TO STUDENTS' LEARNING NEEDS

An additional attribute to which teachers are responsive is students' learning needs. During Lesson Study, teachers analyze data, pinpoint needs, and design learning experiences in response to these needs.

Targeting

Assessment that informs instruction includes informal information that teachers gather in the moment, whenever students are learning. Every interaction with students provides information. Every problem students work, every piece of writing they do, every assignment they complete, is an assessment that can be used to plan future learning. In addition, teachers can create pretests with the express purpose of guiding the lesson planning process.

> For the 1st-grade geometry lesson, Avery, Bethani, and Sarah had come to the Lesson Study planning session described above with data in hand. They had administered a pretest and found that students knew more than they expected about the defining attributes of shapes. Rather than explicitly teaching about all of the attributes, as had been done in the past, they homed in on the two attributes that students hadn't yet mastered: orientation and open/closed. This meant discarding some of the activities they'd discussed at a previous planning meeting. Students just didn't need them. Instead, they thought about how the Smart Board could be used to demonstrate orientation. Students could actually tip and move the shapes and *see* that the shape's identity didn't change. They also talked about how students could intentionally draw a line to close objects that had an open gap, creating familiar shapes.
>
> By focusing on what students needed to know instead of what they already knew, learning moved forward at a more efficient pace. When Avery taught the lesson, students were motivated because they weren't reviewing already-mastered content; they were being stretched with a just-right level of challenge. These teachers didn't just use last year's lesson plan. They adapted it to their current students' needs.

Through ongoing assessment (both formal and informal), teachers gain valuable information that helps them target students' needs as they plan for and enact instruction.

Scaffolding

Making sure instruction is just right for students can also mean providing extra support. We refer to this support as scaffolding—temporary assistance that enables a novice to solve a problem, carry out a task, or achieve a goal that otherwise would be beyond her ability. Scaffolding can be spontaneous or part of lesson design.

Spontaneous scaffolding happens in the moment, as a teacher ascertains a need and seeks to address it. This "in-flight" support requires understanding of learning progressions and an instructional repertoire for supporting this development (Maloch, 2002, p. 110). For example, during a small-group reading lesson, Betsy's 1st-grade students didn't recognize the word *crunch*. Betsy scaffolded in several ways: She reminded students to "rubber band" the word, stretching out the sounds; she encouraged them to use their fingers like elevator doors to isolate parts of the word; and she prompted them to "look at the digraph, the ch, together." Knowing the decoding abilities of the students in this small group, and building on instruction she had previously provided, Betsy scaffolded students' successful decoding of the word (Collet, 2011, p. 121).

Spontaneous scaffolding often occurs individually, as the teacher moves around the room to support students during independent work time. Such support (the Japanese call it "kikan shido," or "between-desks instruction") requires a quick formative assessment of where students are struggling and instant decisionmaking about how to help. Often, this means asking the right question. When Avery saw a 1st-grader stuck on a subtraction problem, she asked, "Can you think of a way to group the objects that might help?" This spontaneous scaffolding moved the student to think differently about the problem, leading to an accurate solution.

During Lesson Study research lessons, observers are alert to teacher moves like these. Talking about them during the debrief adds to teachers' instructional toolkits, helping them be more responsive to their own students. Whether scaffolding is spontaneous or built into the lesson plan, its use represents instruction that is responsive to students' needs. Student learning is contingent upon teachers' moment-by-moment decisionmaking as they plan for and enact responsive instruction.

RESPONSIVENESS TO TEACHERS' NEEDS

An aspect of responsiveness that is seldom considered is responsiveness to teachers' needs. Teachers' own interests, experiences, and values are part of the teaching/learning equation. Plans for instruction will sail or fail based on this alignment. Unenthusiastic teachers provide unenthusiastic instruction, leading to unenthusiastic students. It can't be consistently faked.

A compelling reason for Lesson Study is its influence on teacher engagement. You will feel more mentally active, more appropriately challenged, and more consistently supported as you engage in this collegial process. Lesson Study asks you and your colleagues to identify questions worth pondering. What do you need to know? What are you interested in trying? What do you care about?

These become topics of inquiry for Lesson Study. As you participate, you'll find your interests being expanded and your values being refined, if you keep your mind open. Lesson Study provides new opportunities to listen to and learn from students. And, all the while, student learning improves.

Through Lesson Study, you reduce the insularity of the classroom, bringing your own funds of knowledge to the group. Each teacher is a valuable contributor. You become more aware of the ideologies and practices of those in your teaching community. You engage in collaborative practices that advance your own knowledge and skill as well as that of your colleagues. Your own needs are met as you engage in observation and discussion focused on what you care and wonder about. The collective thinking of your group becomes visible as you consider specific teaching practices. As you work with colleagues, Lesson Study supports continual reimagining—re*Visioning*—of instruction, bringing energy and immediacy to your work.

UNDERSTANDING, FLEXIBILITY, AND RESPONSIVENESS

Teaching must always be dynamically adapted and reinvented to fit the students in your classroom. As you flexibly respond to students' cultures, contexts, interests, and needs, you feel your teaching invigorated. Lesson Study provides a structure for understanding yourself in relation to these aspects of your classroom, for making professional decisions with a mind toward your students' strengths and needs.

During Lesson Study, you have built lessons that have enough breadth and depth for flexibility. You have combined research with insight about your students, and you are able to bend to students' needs. You have built a teaching repertoire from which you can draw appropriate pedagogy for particular purposes with particular groups of students.

Sensitivity to contextual factors is important to school improvement efforts. Educational research has noted that context critically shapes implementation (Gutiérrez & Penuel, 2014; Spillane, Parise, & Sherer, 2011). Lesson Study allows teachers to be contextually responsive and to consider and build upon students' variances and assets.

Vygotsky's ideas about the relationship between learning and development are helpful in explaining why responsiveness is so important. Bodrova and Leong (2007) explain these ideas:

> We cannot make exact prescriptions that produce developmental changes for every child since individual differences are to be expected. We cannot say to a teacher, "If you do this six times, every child will develop a particular skill." The exact relationship between learning and development may be different for each child and for different areas of development. Teachers must constantly adjust their methods to accommodate the learning and teaching process for each child. (p. 11)

Lesson Study participants do this thoughtfully, with understanding of their students' cultures, contexts, interests, and needs. Lesson Study builds routines to detect and learn from variation (Lewis, 2015).

While some have proposed that Lesson Study is the path to a perfected lesson that can be preserved and petrified, my experiences with teachers suggest it's something more. It is a way to build understanding about best practices. It is a way to design instruction that can be flexible, and to support teachers' decisionmaking about that flexibility. It is a way to recognize the importance of being responsive to students. Through Lesson Study, these important insights become part of who we are as teachers, part of what we carry into every classroom, throughout our professional careers.

Reflect and Respond

---

1. **Read** and annotate the following quote:

   > The activities, texts, and expectations of a lesson provide the background circumstances for learning, thus shaping the sociocultural context of the classroom. However, the overall sociocultural context for learning is also shaped by the students' identities and background as learners.
   >
   > —Hassett, 2008, p. 302

   Reflect & Respond: How have students' identities and backgrounds as learners shaped a lesson you have taught or observed?

2. **Read** one of the following:

   - https://tinyurl.com/Ch9-Culture
   - https://www.idra.org/resource-center/three-teaching-strategies/
   - https://www.theedadvocate.org/student-interest-surveys-create-interest/

   Reflect & Respond:

   - Write about a connection you made between what you read on one of these sites and the information in this chapter.

3. **Read** the following quote:

   > Our analysis of funds of knowledge represents a positive (and, we argue, realistic) view of households as containing ample cultural and cognitive resources with great potential utility for classroom instruction.
   >
   > —Moll et al., 2006, p. 134

   Reflect & Respond: How can this view be more fully represented in your teaching?

   Self-Assess: Is there a cultural knowledge gap in your teaching? If so, what are you willing to do to close it?

Ongoing Cycles of Lesson Study

Throughout this book, you've read about the experiences other teachers have had with Lesson Study. You've heard about Kim, Linda, and Allie at Parker Elementary School, and how their collaborative focus on writing helped turn around their school's achievement status. You've read how Ali, Avery, and other preservice teachers at Old Wire Elementary School strengthened their instruction as they planned, observed, and reflected together. From Berryville teachers, you've realized the importance of finding matches between context and instruction. From Lisa, Tasha, and Charity at Stilwell High, you've seen how Lesson Study can tune teachers in to students' cultural resources. I hope stories of these teachers' struggles and strengths have helped you with your own.

By now, I hope you have also had the opportunity to experience the power of Lesson Study for yourself. I hope you have found a few teachers who can gather with you regularly to inquire about best practices for your own students. I hope that Lesson Study will become part of how you do school, that it will continue to be part of your professional experiences long after you finish reading this book. You can return to these pages for insight and support as you experience the Lesson Study cycle again and again. As you study, plan, observe, reflect, re*Vision*, and reteach, your understanding will increase, and you'll be able to be more flexible and responsive to the students who walk through your classroom door each day. This book concludes with suggestions for making each part of the Lesson Study cycle an ongoing element of your quest for continuous instructional improvement.

VARIATIONS AND ITERATIONS

Since its beginnings in Japan, Lesson Study has been taken up all over the world. With this diffusion has come variation. In some iterations, for example, Lesson Study includes only the final stages of the cycle I've described, omitting the initial phases of study and planning and jumping right in with observation, sometimes of a video-recorded lesson. Sometimes the emphasis is on taking preplanned lessons, teaching them, reflecting, and revising for the good of the group. Lesson Study has occurred in small groups of teachers meeting face-to-face, in large groups sitting in front of a giant screen, and in online communities. Of necessity, Lesson Study has been adapted to meet local needs. However, my hope is that you will find ways to retain each phase of the Lesson Study cycle you've read about in this book. Each part offers insight for instructional improvement. Hopefully, you'll be able to experience each part of the cycle with at least one teaching colleague. That is the ideal. There's so much power in collaboration! As circumstances change, you may want to reread Chapter 2 for ideas about how to make time for collaboration. But no matter how many like-minded colleagues you find to walk the Lesson Study journey with you, you can make it happen for yourself continuously. Just as flexibility is important in teaching, it is necessary if Lesson Study is to be an ongoing part of your practice, an approach you take with you wherever you go. You can decide now to make all six stages of Lesson Study part of your work for the rest of your professional teaching life.

Study

Your professional bookshelf is a good starting place for your study of best practices to incorporate through Lesson Study. The books that have inspired you in the past can be resources to energize your teaching. Your school library may have a section for teachers you can also draw from, and university libraries are full of reference materials. When it comes to finding research on a specific topic, Google Scholar can be a helpful tool (scholar.google.com). Recently I was working with a team of 3rd-grade teachers in a Lesson Study cycle on teaching elapsed time. A regular Google search provided lots of teaching suggestions, but a Google Scholar search pointed us to which practices were supported by research. From that site we found an article specific to this topic (Kamii & Russell, 2012) and another that gave insights about leading an inquiry discussion on a math topic (Smith et al., 2009). These resources got our planning off to a good start.

Whether you are studying alone or with colleagues, it is important to move beyond the cute and clever printables you may find online and the prescriptive lessons that may be suggested through curricular resources. Study will help you identify core principles that should guide your lesson.

Plan

During planning, you shape a vision for your lesson. Drawing on a range of resources helps you create richer learning experiences. Like a gem that refracts light, you can hold a potential lesson activity up for consideration, turning it this way and that, thinking about it from the perspective of different students in your classes. How will they respond? Close examination will help you decide which activities earn their way into your lesson plan.

As you plan, consider how students' thinking will be made visible. What will students do, say, and write that will give you windows to their understanding? When you lean toward teaching experiences that make students' thinking observable, you are also building lessons that increase and elevate the thinking students are doing. Your purposeful planning enriches the learning experience.

Observe

As Mitch Nobis of Red Cedar Writing Project exclaimed (National Writing Project, 2018), observing a lesson or having someone observe you teach is like professional development on steroids! The more eyes you have on students as they learn, the more information you'll collect about their learning. This is one of the reasons why the observation phase of the Lesson Study cycle is so important. But even when you are on your own, observing your own students day in and day out in your classroom, the pre-observation practices described in Chapter 5 can make watching your students more insightful.

As you think through your lesson in advance to make sure you're ready to teach, anticipate students' responses and how you might proceed if that happens. Doing so will open your eyes to students' understandings and their misconceptions as they play out during the lesson.

Reflect

I love the poem "A Lazy Thought" by Eve Merriam (2005, p. 10), which reminds me about the tempo needed for growth. After describing the rush of grownups' lives, she ends with the phrase, "It takes a lot of slow to grow."

After describing the rush of grownups' lives, she ends with the phrase, "It takes a lot of slow to grow." It takes a lot of slow for children to grow and learn, and I'm of the belief that the same axiom is true for teachers. As teachers, we need to create for ourselves opportunities to slow down and reflect on the teaching-learning process. Because of the hurried, packed-full nature of teachers' days, it is essential that we build in opportunities to pause and ponder, to reflect and refine. When do you routinely reflect on your teaching day, alone or with colleagues? These times are a necessity, not a luxury. They fuel the cycle of improvement.

ReVision

Planning creates a vision for instruction. During observation, you see that plan in action. And then reflection helps you reVision your practice, seeing new opportunities. When you reVision, you think first about the single lesson, the one you and your team so carefully crafted. But as you reflect together, your view rises above the specificities of this particular day, this particular content. You are able to see how practices apply across a variety of settings. You learn, for example, how the pregnant pause of wait time gives birth to new student insights. You come to understand how giving students too much support robs them of the opportunity to figure things out for themselves. Principles like these are elevated through close examination.

Re*Visioning* means seeing yourselves, your students, your teaching, and their learning in a new light because of your careful attention throughout the Lesson Study process. You re*Vision* your teaching in ways that make sense culturally and contextually for you and your students. You gain insight about what works and foresight about how it will work with your students, and you are able to flexibly apply this understanding in future lessons.

Reteach

Reteaching gives you the opportunity to put your hunches and hypotheses to the test. If a lesson didn't initially meet your objectives, you might re*Vision* the lesson and teach it again to the same group of students. As a secondary teacher, you might re*Vision* a lesson before teaching it to the next group of students, and then slightly re*Vision* it before teaching it to another. Reteaching might mean saving the revised lesson plan for next year, when you teach similar content. In a broad sense, the re*Visioning* work you do becomes part of your vision for every lesson moving forward.

Mandates and curriculum may leave you feeling restricted, but you almost always have more freedom than you may recognize. The nuances of moment-by-moment instructional decisionmaking provide opportunities to enact your vision for effective instruction.

DISPOSITIONS

In addition to the processes of Lesson Study that you'll take with you into the future, I hope that reading this book has increased your awareness of dispositions that support and enrich your professional work. I hope that you are more inclined to collaborate, inquire, and teach responsively and for deep understanding, because these dispositions invigorate your work and make it more impactful.

Collaboration

Lesson Study is an important shift away from teacher isolation. By making teaching public and collaborative, Lesson Study provides opportunities for teachers to share, solve problems together, and inspire one another to grow as teachers and learners. The Lesson Study process has the potential to support sharing across grade-level teams, departments, schools, districts, and even more broadly, as Lesson Study networks develop. Making the work collaborative builds collective efficacy and shared responsibility for student learning.

Teaching is improved when it is a professional interaction rather than a solitary exercise. Working with your peers, you deepen your own knowledge.

Sharing your practice can have an immediate, productive impact on pedagogy. As you open your door and teach, and then reflect with others, you learn through the complexity and messiness of your real context. As you talk with another teacher, you think about what happened in ways that haven't occurred to you until you put it into words. You see the work differently. You re*Vision* your practice.

Inquiry

Lesson Study creates a forum for authentic learning through teacher inquiry. You are conducting action research as you identify a problem or focus, consider previous work, plan a lesson built on hypotheses of how students will respond, teach the lesson, analyze the results, and determine implications.

What are you wondering about as you plan the next unit or think about your growth as a teacher? Make these questions a focus for personal or collective investigation. As you examine questions directly related to your context, this mental work will invigorate you and your teaching.

Responsiveness

As a teacher, you use a variety of resources to make instructional decisions that are aligned to the needs, interests, cultures, and contexts of your students and classes. Because I want to keep all those aspects in mind throughout the Lesson Study process, I have printed a reminder that says, "Consider context, culture, and students' interests and needs" in the biggest font that will fit on a single piece of paper. I take that paper out and put it in the middle of the table whenever I am doing Lesson Study work with a team of teachers. It helps us keep our kids at the forefronts of our minds as we study, plan, observe, reflect, and re*Vision*.

Through Lesson Study, you learn from variation. The insights you gain as you look at particulars can be applied in quite different contexts. Contrasts within and between contexts illuminate unrecognized assumptions and provide opportunities to expand your understanding.

Reflection

Lesson Study sets aside time to thoughtfully revisit instruction. Having a disposition for reflection helps us properly judge. When you revisit your classroom in your mind, reflect on individual students and how they responded during the lesson. Knowing students as learners helps you plan and teach in increasingly responsive ways.

As you go beyond instinctive reactions and logically consider your teaching and students' learning, be generous with yourself and celebrate successes, large and small. You will grow as you recognize what went right and do it more consistently. Your habit of considering successes and less successful aspects of the lesson supports increased understanding and ongoing improvement.

Understanding

Lesson Study supports teaching for understanding as you plan toward big ideas in the discipline that you want students to grasp and the learning experiences that will lead there. When students are active participants, they make discoveries that stay with them in the form of concepts rather than easily forgotten facts. What have you discovered about teaching that leads to student understanding?

For teachers, understanding develops as you contemplate your content, your students, and their responses to instruction and as you engage in deep conversations with colleagues about instructional practice. As you articulate what practices matter most and why, the insights you gain transcend the research lesson and guide your future teaching self.

RE*VISIONING* THROUGH LESSON STUDY

Research in the United States shows that when the supports provided by Lesson Study are made available to teachers, "they are able to improve their knowledge, to build habits and dispositions that support improvement" (Lewis et al., 2012, p. 368). Lesson Study helps teachers develop and maintain a stance of flexibility, recognizing that teaching is improvable but not perfectible. Although the products of Lesson Study, such as annotated lessons, are important, the process of Lesson Study is valuable because of its ability to support teachers' professional development.

Lesson Study provides job-embedded, practice-based professional learning that improves student achievement (Collet, 2017; Dudley, 2012; Gersten et al., 2014; Lewis et al., 2006). It is a conceptually simple but powerful process that benefits teachers and students. Because it is situated at the classroom level, Lesson Study has a direct, positive impact on student learning. To reiterate Guskey's (2005) findings, it doesn't really matter what national or district reform movements are adopted. It is what happens at the building and classroom levels that matters. Although mandates may be put in place, educational change really happens at the local level.

Reform efforts usually have an emphasis on accountability. Lesson Study includes structures that naturally lead to accountability—accountability to colleagues rather than external measures, and accountability to students, the customers of instruction. Teachers care about the students who file into their classrooms every day. Having a process for working with colleagues impacts kids.

The Lesson Study process builds professional learning communities (PLCs) or makes them better. The teachers at Stilwell High, who had received extensive training in PLCs, called Lesson Study the missing piece. Through this process of collaborative inquiry, they built professional understanding that helped them respond to their students in ways that built students' understanding.

As teachers collaboratively study, plan, observe, reflect, re*Vision*, and reteach, they are empowered to improve their craft. Classrooms are data-rich places, and Lesson Study offers structures for evaluating practice in the midst of these spaces. It is job-embedded work, not one-off training. Instead of being presented with new ideas, teachers create them. Teachers are producers, not merely consumers, of curriculum and professional best practices. They are drivers of their own learning, engaged in a continuous cycle of professional development.

Lesson Study uses knowledge you gain from your own classroom to stimulate professional conversations about teaching and learning. Shared experiences through joint planning and observation support the conversation, helping you develop your own understanding and share it with others.

As you think about next steps, I hope you will be eager to investigate and improve instruction and increase your understanding about teaching. Advocate for collaborative professional experiences like Lesson Study in your school or district or through local professional organizations. The Lesson Study cycle expounded in this book creates a climate for ongoing growth and re*Visioning* of practice that values teaching and teachers, learning and students.

Reflect and Respond

---

1. ***Read*** and annotate the following quote:

> In order to establish schools in which inter-dependence and collaboration are the new norm, we must create the structures and cultures that embed collaboration in the routine practice of our schools, ensure that the collaborative efforts focus on the right work, and support educators as they build their capacity to work together rather than alone.
>
> —DuFour, 2004, in Patterson & Tolnay, 2015, p. 7

Reflect & Respond: How are the criteria DuFour outlines exemplified in Lesson Study?

2. ***Read or watch*** one of the following:

   - https://tinyurl.com/Concl-Lesson-Study-Benefits
   - https://tinyurl.com/Concl-Lesson-Study-in-Zambia
   - https://tinyurl.com/Concl-Lesson-Study

Reflect & Respond: How do the benefits of Lesson Study described in the items above match up with your experiences?

3. ***Read*** the following quote:

> The writer must have a good imagination to begin with, but the imagination has to be muscular, which means it must be exercised in a disciplined way, day in and day out, by writing, failing, succeeding and revising.
>
> —Stephen King in Strawser, 2009, p. 48

Reflect & Respond: Apply this quote about writing to teaching. How is teachers' imagination made muscular through Lesson Study?

Self-Assess: Read the following quote:

We were revisionists; what we revised was ourselves.

—Margaret Atwood, 1986, p. 227

Reflect & Respond: In what ways are you revising yourself or re*Visioning* your teaching through participation in Lesson Study?

Agenda for Introducing Lesson Study

by Savanna Gragg

Materials: Chart paper with three-column K-W-L chart, sticky notes, copies of Stigler & Hiebert quote for each participant, copies of articles (see below).

1. K-W-L Chart

    • Participants respond on sticky notes to the prompt, "What do you know or want to know about Lesson Study?"
    • Put sticky notes on K-W-L chart.

2. Quote Response

    > Improving something as complex and culturally embedded as teaching requires the efforts of all the players, including students, parents, and politicians. But teachers must be the primary driving force behind change. They are best positioned to understand the problems that students face and to generate possible solutions.
    > —James Stigler & James Hiebert, 1999, p. 135

    • Participants read and annotate the quote.
    • Participants reflect on what the quote means to them individually.
    • Turn and talk about the quote.

3. Article/Podcast/Video

    • Participants choose one of the resources below about Lesson Study and listen/view/read with these two objectives:
        ➤ What is Lesson Study?
        ➤ What is the process/cycle for conducting Lesson Study?
    • Group discussion: Define Lesson Study.

4. Group Illustration

    • Work in small groups to illustrate the Lesson Study process on chart paper.
    • Small groups report.
    • Discuss similarities and differences.

5. K-W-L Chart Revisited

- Move sticky notes from "What to Know" to "Know" column, as appropriate.
- Add new stickies to "Know" column.
- Address remaining "Want to Knows" as appropriate; plan to address remaining questions in the future.

6. Journal Prompt

- Write for 3 minutes about the implication of Lesson Study for you as a teacher. Rate yourself on a 1–5 scale, with 1 being "I know nothing about Lesson Study" to 5, "I know what I need to know to get started."

Articles/Podcast/Video

American Radio Works. (2015, August). Teaching teachers [Audio podcast]. Retrieved from http://www.americanradioworks.org/documentaries/teaching-teachers/Partial transcription available at http://www.americanradioworks.org/segments/a-different-approach-to-teacher-learning-lesson-study/

Lewis, C. C., Perry, R. R., Friedkin, S., & Roth, J. R. (2012). Improving teaching does improve teachers: Evidence from Lesson Study. *Journal of Teacher Education, 63*(5), 368–375.

Lewis, C. C. (2010, September 29). Japan's Lesson Study [Video]. Retrieved from https://www.youtube.com/watch?v=0xgko79kO94

Lewis, C., Perry, R., & Hurd, J. (2004). A deeper look at lesson study. *Educational Leadership, 61*(5), 18–23.

Planning Our Lesson

Topic:

Standard(s):

Definitions:

Student-Friendly Objective:

KUDs (What will students <u>K</u>now, <u>U</u>nderstand, and be able to <u>D</u>o):

What do students already know about this topic? What evidence do we have of this knowledge? (Consider context, culture, and students' interests and needs.)

What misconceptions might students have? (Consider context, culture, and students' interests and needs.)

What might motivate students to learn about this topic? (Consider context, culture, and students' interests and needs.)

What curriculum resources do we have for teaching this topic?

What other resources are available? (Consider context, culture, and students' interests and needs.)

What does research have to say about teaching this topic?

What learning experiences might help students develop understanding of this topic? (Consider context, culture, and students' interests and needs.)

How might students respond to these experiences? (Consider context, culture, and students' interests and needs.)

How could the teacher respond to these student responses? (Consider context, culture, and students' interests and needs.)

Design a data collection plan.

Observation Day Agenda

5th-Grade Literacy Lesson
Berryville Intermediate School

Introduction & Lesson Overview (10:15–11:00)

TOPIC: Notice and Note—Contrasts/Contradictions and "Aha" Moments

- Why was this topic selected?
  - What do we notice about 5th-graders as readers?
  - What is difficult about teaching/learning this topic?
- What are our wonderings about this topic?
- Complete Lesson Design Template
- Context for Observation Classroom
- Data Collection Plan
  - What data will help us understand student progress?
  - What is the best way to collect these data (photos, chart paper, notes, chart, etc.)?
  - Who will collect each type of data?

Lesson Teaching/Observation (11:00–11:40)

- Please do not talk to one another or to students or teacher.
- Lean in to listen.
- Shift your focus.
- Take nonevaluative notes (use your senses).

Reflect (11:40–12:40)

- Review notes and highlight anything that seems important.
- Return to Lesson Design chart.
  - Complete "What did we notice?" and "Why is this important?" for each activity.
  - Report on other data.

Re *Vision* (12:40–1:30)

- What should we keep?
- What should we modify?
- What should we discard?

Closure

- What instructional strategies do we want to be sure to use in future instruction?
- What big ideas are we taking with us?
- What can we do to make Lesson Study more meaningful in our next round?

Hopefully, the lesson will not go exactly as planned. If the outcome is exactly what we expected, we have not really learned anything—we have just reinforced what we already knew!

Videos for Observation Practice

Using the video links below, you can practice note-taking before observing your research lesson.

Kindergarten English

> https://www.youtube.com/watch?v=0xF2rklvyFo
> https://www.youtube.com/watch?v=NIk1-ck4c6Q

2nd-grade fractions

> https://www.youtube.com/watch?v=KRgIxK0WNis

Elementary poetry

> https://www.youtube.com/watch?v=L9FuNZspeAI

3rd-grade science

> https://www.youtube.com/watch?v=J4G2DT1MBPY

4th-grade math

> https://www.youtube.com/watch?v=Nw4R3HwwiUY

Middle school language arts

> https://www.youtube.com/watch?v=qHaq7CTV4pE

Middle school math

> https://www.youtube.com/watch?v=VVh3Ty6nZ5M

Middle school science

> https://www.youtube.com/watch?v=tChbmFBcYKg

5th-grade language arts

https://www.youtube.com/watch?v=O88ifgdcSRQ

High school math

https://www.youtube.com/watch?v=CH4IMgEM9og
https://www.youtube.com/watch?v=Qkl_KcyY3kM
https://www.youtube.com/watch?v=h6WJdsb0dfM

Algebra 1

https://www.youtube.com/watch?v=FAgT1NaDdq8

High school English

https://www.youtube.com/watch?v=pgk-719mTxM

9th-grade biology

https://www.youtube.com/watch?v=g9kyl_WPFhU

Before and After Lesson Study Plans

Lesson Study doesn't require a special lesson plan format—use whatever template you are comfortable with. Below are "Before" and "After" lesson plans that demonstrate how the Lesson Study cycle refines instruction.

1ST-GRADE SHAPE ATTRIBUTES LESSON PLAN (BEFORE OBSERVATION)

Title/Subject: Defining and Nondefining Attributes of Shapes

Standard: Distinguish between defining attributes (e.g., triangles are closed and three-sided) versus nondefining attributes (e.g., color, orientation, overall size); build and draw shapes to possess defining attributes.

Student-Friendly Objective: I can describe attributes that define a shape.

KUDs:

Know: An attribute is a way to describe a shape.
Understand: Shapes have specific attributes that make them what they are; some attributes are not relevant to naming shapes.
Do: Distinguish between defining and nondefining attributes; sort based on attributes.

Procedures (includes preplanned questions):

Schema Activation: Show abstract art on Smart Board and have students find shapes (Jaime Rovenstine, 2012) (5–7 minutes).

Next Steps: Show three shapes with differing attributes on Smart Board, asking open-ended questions about the shapes (10 minutes).

- Do this as a teacher-directed discussion, not showing the video.
- Create an anchor chart of attributes (how/when to distinguish between defining and nondefining?). Include visuals for each attribute.

Use shapes on the Smart Board to demonstrate that open and closed is a defining attribute (5 minutes).

- Slide with open and closed figures—what do you notice?
- Slide with mixed open and closed figures to sort.
- Describe that this is a defining attribute.

Use shapes on Smart Board to demonstrate that orientation is not a defining attribute (5 minutes).

- Note that orientation is a defining attribute for letters and numbers but not for people and objects.

Play "What's the Rule" game, calling on a few students to say why they put their card in the circle or left it out (10 minutes).

- T lays out two cards that have the same attribute.
  - ➢ T chose sets that share both defining and nondefining attributes.
- Ss put their card down if it shares the attribute.
- Have a few share why they put their card down or didn't.
  - ➢ After each shares justification, thumbs up or down in regards to defining or nondefining.
- Partner talk about why they did or did not put down for a couple of turns.

Optional Extension: Explain a shape to a partner using attributes (probably won't have time for this).

- Describer should draw it first, then they can compare when done.
- Use attributes list to help them give enough/good clues.

Closure: T describes a shape using only defining features and has Ss think about one nondefining feature that they get to choose and use in their drawing.

Student Self-Evaluation: Do you think you could draw a shape and describe it to your partner so that they could draw it, using defining and nondefining attributes?

REVISED 1ST-GRADE SHAPE ATTRIBUTES LESSON PLAN
(AFTER OBSERVATION; CHANGES/ADDITIONS ARE IN BOLD)

Title/Subject: Defining and Nondefining Attributes of Shapes

Standard: Distinguish between defining attributes (e.g., triangles are closed and three-sided) versus nondefining attributes (e.g., color, orientation, overall size); build and draw shapes to possess defining attributes.

Student-Friendly Objective: I can describe attributes that define a shape.

KUDs:

Know: An attribute is a way to describe a shape.
Understand: Shapes have specific attributes that make them what they are; some attributes are not relevant to naming shapes.
Do: Distinguish between defining and nondefining attributes; sort based on attributes.

Procedures (includes preplanned questions):

Schema Activation: Show abstract art on Smart Board and have students find shapes (Jaime Rovenstine, 2012) (5–7 minutes). **Students use the Smart Board pen to trace shapes in the art.**

- **Model tracing a shape in the artwork.**
- **Ask: What shapes do you see?**
- **Ask: What *big* shapes do you see?**
- **Ask additional questions as needed (support vocabulary): Do you see squares? Do you see rectangles? Do you see triangles? Do you see circles?**

Next Steps: Show three shapes with differing attributes on Smart Board, asking open-ended questions about the shapes (10 minutes).

- Do this as a teacher-directed discussion, not showing the video.
- **Create an anchor chart of attributes.**
  - ➤ **T-chart with headings "Defining/Nondefining" (explain headings).**
    - ✓ **Encourage Ss to ask themselves, "Would that change my shape?" (If it would change the shape, it is *defining*.)**
    - ✓ **When Ss mention size, ask questions to help students understand that a shape can change from a square to a rectangle by changing the length of some sides differently**

- o **Use Smart Board to manipulate shapes and demonstrate.**
  - ✓ **Students chorally repeat the words *defining* and *nondefining*.**
- ➤ **As attributes are mentioned, ask students questions to determine whether the attribute is defining or nondefining (e.g., Would it still be a triangle if it were blue?).**
- ➤ **Include visuals for each attribute.**

Use shapes on Smart Board to demonstrate that open and closed is a defining attribute (5 minutes).

- • Slide with open and closed figures—what do you notice?
  - ➤ **Draw a letter c.**
  - ➤ **Ask: Is there a letter similar to c but closed?**
  - ➤ **Just like letters, shapes are defined by whether they are open or closed.**
  - ➤ **If we can drive all the way around the edge and keep on going, it is a closed shape.**
- • **Slide with mixed open and closed figures to sort.**
  - ➤ **Ss come individually to board, taking turns sorting objects.**
  - ➤ **All respond: agree or disagree (thumbs up or down).**
- • Describe that this is a defining attribute.

Use shapes on Smart Bboard to demonstrate that orientation is not a defining attribute (5 minutes).

- • Note that orientation is a defining attribute for letters and numbers but not for people and objects.
- • **Use a right triangle for one of the examples.**

Play "What's the Rule" game, calling on a few students to say why they put their card in the circle or left it out (10 minutes).

- • T lays out two cards that have the same attribute.
  - ➤ T chose sets that share both defining and nondefining attributes.
  - ➤ **T models several examples.**
  - ➤ **Start with simple example, like square and circle, that are different colors and sizes (attribute = shared # of sides).**
- • Ss put their card down if it shares the attribute.
- • Have a few share why they put card down or didn't.
  - ➤ After each shares justification, thumbs up or down in regard to defining or nondefining.

- Partner talk about why they did or did not put down for a couple of turns.

Extension: Explain a shape to a partner using attributes **(prepare to include this activity)**.

- Describer should draw it first, then they can compare when done.
- Use attributes list to help them give enough/good clues.

Closure: T describes a shape using only defining features and has them think about one nondefining feature that they get to choose and use in their drawing.

Student Self-Evaluation: Do you think you could draw a shape and describe it to your partner so that they could draw it, using defining and nondefining attributes?

5TH-GRADE ECOSYSTEMS LESSON PLAN
(BEFORE OBSERVATION)

Title/Subject: Ecosystems

Learning Goals/Objectives:

Standard: Develop a model to describe the movement of matter among plants, animals, decomposers, and the environment.

(What do you want your students to KNOW, UNDERSTAND, and BE ABLE TO DO as a result of this lesson?)

- Organisms can survive only in environments in which their particular needs are met.
  - ➤ I can explain the relationships between organisms in their ecosystem.

What do students already know about this topic? What evidence do we have of this knowledge?

- Relationships between organisms such as symbiotic
- Food chains (primary, secondary, tertiary creatures)
- Some understanding of biomes

Materials:

- Video
- Laptops
- Resources (websites) and pictures of plants and animals
- Colored paper
- Graphic organizer

Procedures (includes preplanned questions):

Schema Activation: The students will (TSW) watch video (*The Lion King*) to make observations about the environment and the interactions between animals: https://www.youtube.com/watch?v=bW7PlTaawfQ

Next Steps: (Before the video) The teacher will (TTW) have the students get out a piece of paper and write down the definitions as we discuss them of the important words that will better help us understand how to solve the problem.

TTW have the students grab a laptop and put it on their desks.

TTW ask the students: What is a community? (put on anchor chart)

TTW ask students: How can we define population? (put on anchor chart)

TTW explain that these concepts will help us understand ecosystems. TTW ask the students to define *ecosystem*: living and nonliving things that interact with one another in a specific environment.

TTW ask: If you listen to the word *interdependence*, what do you think it means? TSW discuss the meaning of the word and how it may be important in ecosystems (put on anchor chart).

TTW pose the problem that a natural disaster shook up the world, and animals and plants are in the wrong ecosystems. The students have the challenge to do research to determine where certain animals and plants should be and why.

Each group gets an envelope with things that belong and don't belong in their ecosystem. TSW research to determine these organisms and their interdependencies. TSW complete a 4-square graphic organizer for their ecosystem (plants, animals, climate, hazards). TSW glue on the organisms that belong to their poster.

TSW be given time to research the animals, plants, and characteristics of their particular ecosystem. As students complete their posters, they will put them up around the room.

When students complete their posters, the class will do a carousel walk. TSW walk around to each ecosystem and then write an aspect about the ecosystems' climate, animals, and plants on their graphic organizers and hazards.

Closure: Class discussion to compare and contrast some different ecosystems to further define what an ecosystem must include and why, as well as some consequences of some sort of interference to the ecosystems' natural order.

Differentiation:

- Student interest will be incorporated into the lesson through video, technology, and student interest in the different ecosystems.
- ELLs will be supported through visuals, definitions, and student collaboration.
- Students will be grouped strategically to support learning and participation.

Evaluation:

Evaluation criteria: Students will meet the goal of the lesson if they are able to identify the attributes of a specific ecosystem and its interdependent parts. The students will also be able to discuss the outcomes of what would happen if something interfered with the ecosystems' natural order.

Student Self-Assessment: At the bottom of the students' graphic organizers, they will be instructed to consider the self-evaluation criteria on the wall of the classroom. Students will be asked to record their level of understanding and confidence regarding the learning objective. If they have concerns, they can include them there.

REVISED 5TH-GRADE ECOSYSTEMS LESSON PLAN (AFTER OBSERVATION; ADDITIONS ARE BOLDED; DELETIONS HAVE STRIKE-THROUGHS)

Title/Subject: Ecosystems

Learning Goals/Objectives:

Standard: Develop a model to describe the movement of matter among plants, animals, decomposers, and the environment.

(What do you want your students to KNOW, UNDERSTAND, and BE ABLE TO DO as a result of this lesson?)

- Organisms can survive only in environments in which their particular needs are met.
  - ➤ I can explain the relationships between organisms in their ecosystem.

What do students already know about this topic? What evidence do we have of this knowledge?

- Relationships between organisms such as symbiotic
- Food chains (primary, secondary, tertiary creatures)
- Some understanding of biomes

Materials:

- Video
- Laptops
- Resources (websites) and pictures of plants and animals
- Colored paper
- Graphic organizer

Procedures (includes preplanned questions):

Schema Activation: TSW watch video (*The Lion King*) to make observations about the environment and the interactions between animals: https://www.youtube.com/watch?v=bW7PlTaawfQ

Next Steps: (Before the video) TTW have the students get out a piece of paper and write down the definitions as we discuss them of the important words that will better help us understand how to solve the problem.

TTW have the students grab a laptop and put it on their desks.

TTW ask the students: What is a community? (put on anchor chart)

TTW ask students: How can we define population? (put on anchor chart)

TTW explain that these concepts will help us understand ecosystems. TTW ask the students to define *ecosystem*: living and nonliving things that interact with one another in a specific environment (put on anchor chart).

TTW ask: If you listen to the word *interdependence*, what do you think it means? TSW discuss the meaning of the word and how it may be important in ecosystems (put on anchor chart).

TTW pose the problem that **a series of natural disasters (tornadoes, floods, hurricanes, tsunamis, volcanic eruptions, earthquakes, storms, famines, and wildfires)** shook up the world, and animals and plants are in the wrong ecosystems. The students have the challenge to do research to determine where certain animals and plants should be and why. **Tell them they are researchers. Make it feel like a real scenario and a real problem they are trying to solve. Describe how all the ecosystems got mixed up.**

Each group gets an envelope with things that belong and don't belong in their ecosystem. TSW research to determine these organisms and their interdependencies. **Emphasize to students that because of the natural disaster, there are things in their envelope that don't belong in their ecosystem. They have to figure out what needs to be included or removed from their ecosystem so that it will be in balance.** Students complete a four-square graphic organizer for their ecosystem (plants, animals, climate, hazards).

Students should then draw the organisms that belong in their ecosystem on their poster, along with a background that illustrates the type of ecosystem.
TSW be given time to research the animals, plants, and characteristics of their particular ecosystem. As students complete their posters, they will put them up around the room. **Provide a list of helpful websites. Encourage them as they use additional websites to check the validity of the source.**
When students complete their posters, the class will do a carousel walk. TSW walk around to each ecosystem and then write an aspect of the ecosystems' climate, animals, plants, and hazards **on their graphic organizers for each ecosystem.**

Closure: Class discussion to compare and contrast some different ecosystems to further define what an ecosystem must include and why, as well as some consequences of some sort of interference to the ecosystems' natural order. **How are the parts of your ecosystem interdependent? What would happen if something interfered with the ecosystems' natural order? Why is the biome important for the ecosystem to be the way it is?**

Differentiation:

- Student interest will be incorporated into the lesson through video, technology, and student interest in the different ecosystems.
- ELLs will be supported through visuals, definitions, and student collaboration.
- Students will be grouped strategically to support learning and participation.

Evaluation:

Evaluation criteria: Students will meet the goal of the lesson if they are able to identify the attributes of a specific ecosystem and its interdependent parts. The students will also be able to discuss the outcomes of what would happen if something interfered with the ecosystems' natural order.

Student Self-Assessment: At the bottom of the students' graphic organizers, they will be instructed to consider the self-evaluation criteria on the wall of the classroom. Students will be asked to record their level of understanding and confidence regarding the learning objective. If they have concerns, they can include them there.

Student Interest Inventory

What are your favorite things to do at home?

What clubs, groups, teams, or organizations do you belong to?

Is there something you like to collect?

What's something you know a lot about?

If you had a million dollars, what would you do with it?

If you could have one wish, what would it be?

List three words that describe you:

——————————, ——————————, ——————————

List the adults who live with you:

Who else lives in your home?

What language(s) do you speak?

If you could learn about anything you wanted to, what would it be?

What is your favorite activity or subject in school? Why is it your favorite?

In school, I learn best when working:
☐ alone   ☐ with one other person
☐ in a small group   ☐ in a larger group
What else would you like me to know about you?

References

Ageyev, V. S. (2003). Vygotsky in the mirror of cultural interpretations. In A. Kozulin, B. Gindis, V. Ageyev, & S. Miller (Eds.), *Vygotsky's educational theory in cultural context* (pp. 432–449). Cambridge, UK: Cambridge University Press.

Allegretto, S., Corcoran, S., & Mishel, L. (2004). *How does teacher pay compare? Methodological challenges and answers.* Washington, DC: Economic Policy Institute.

Amobi, F. A. (2005). Preservice teachers' reflectivity on the sequence and consequences of teaching actions in a microteaching experience. *Teacher Education Quarterly, 32*(1), 115–126.

Appell, E. (1979). "And then the day came." Retrieved from http://anaisninblog. skybluepress.com/2013/03/who-wrote-risk-is-the-mystery-solved/

Atwood, M. (1986). *The handmaid's tale.* New York, NY: Houghton Mifflin Harcourt.

Auman, M. (2003). *Step up to writing* (2nd ed.). Longmont, CO: Sopris West.

Barth, R. S. (2006). Improving relationships within the schoolhouse. *Educational Leadership, 63*(6), 8–13.

Bascia, N. (2014). *The school context model: How school environments shape students' opportunities to learn.* Toronto, Ontario, Canada: Measuring What Matters: People for Education.

Bean, R., & Lillenstein, J. (2012). Response to intervention and the changing roles of schoolwide personnel. *The Reading Teacher, 65*(7), 491–501.

Beta, T. (2010). *Betelgeuse incident: Insiden bait Al-Jauza.* Jakarta, Indonesia: Bumi Intitama Sejahtera.

Bieda, K. N., Cavanna, J., & Ji, X. (2015). Mentor-guided lesson study as a tool to support learning in field experiences. *Mathematics Teacher Educator, 4*(1), 20–31.

Bingham, T., & Conner, M. (2015). *The new social learning: Connect. Collaborate. Work* (2nd ed.). Alexandria, VA: Association for Talent Development.

Blair, W. M. (1957, November 15). President draws planning moral: Recalls army days to show value of preparedness in time of crisis. *The New York Times,* p. 4.

Blank, R. K., de las Alas, N., & Smith, C. (2008). *Does teacher professional development have effects on teaching and learning? Analysis of evaluation findings from programs for mathematics and science teachers in 14 states.* Washington, DC: The Council of Chief State School Officers. Retrieved from http://www.ccsso.org/projects/improving_ evaluation_of_professional_development/

Bocala, C. (2015). From experience to expertise: The development of teachers' learning in lesson study. *Journal of Teacher Education, 66*(4), 349–362.

Bodrova, E., & Leong, D. J. (2007). *Tools of the mind: The Vygotskian approach to early childhood education.* Upper Saddle River, NJ: Pearson Prentice Hall.

Bowman-Perrott, L., Davis, H., Vannest, K., Williams, L., Greenwood, C., & Parker, R. (2013). Academic benefits of peer tutoring: A meta-analytic review of single-case research. *School Psychology Review, 42*(1), 39–55.

Bransford, J. D., Brown, A. L., & Cocking, R. R. (2000). *How people learn: Brain, mind, experience, and school.* Washington, DC: National Academy Press.

Bruce, C. D., Esmonde, I., Ross, J., Dookie, L., & Beatty, R. (2010). The effects of sustained classroom-embedded teacher professional learning on teacher efficacy and related student achievement. *Teaching and Teacher Education, 26*(8), 1598–1608.

Bryk, A. S., Gomez, L. M., Grunow, A., & LeMahieu, P. (2015). *Learning to improve: How America's schools can get better at getting better.* Cambridge, MA: Harvard Education Press.

Buckner, A. (n.d.). Mentor texts for organizing writing. Available at https://choiceliteracy.com/article/mentor-texts-for-organizing-writing/.

Butler, D. L., & Schnellert, L. (2012). Collaborative inquiry in teacher professional development. *Teaching and Teacher Education, 28,* 1206–1220.

Caires, S., & Almeida, L. S. (2007). Positive aspects of the teacher training supervision: The student teachers' perspective. *European Journal of Psychology of Education, 22*(4), 515–528.

Calkins, L. (2013). *Units of study in opinion, information, and narrative writing.* Portsmouth, NH: Heinemann.

Carey, J. (2001). *Kushiel's dart.* New York, NY: Tom Doherty Associates.

Carpenter, T. P. (2014). *Children's mathematics: Cognitively Guided Instruction.* Portsmouth, NH: Heinemann.

Celio, C. I., Durlak, J., & Dymnicki, A. (2011). A meta-analysis of the impact of service-learning on students. *Journal of Experiential Education, 34*(2), 164–181.

Chetty, R., Friedman, J. N., & Rockoff, J. E. (2011). *The long-term impacts of teachers: Teacher value-added and student outcomes in adulthood* (No. w17699). Cambridge, MA: National Bureau of Economic Research.

Chun, H., & Dickson, G. (2011). A psychoecological model of academic performance among Hispanic adolescents. *Journal of Youth and Adolescence, 40*(12), 1581–1594.

Ciminelli, M., Collet, V. S., Baldassarre Hopkins, M., Ames Knips, M., Lee, S. J., Montgomery, C. R., et al. (2009, April). *The impact of No Child Left Behind on diverse stakeholders in education.* Paper presented at the annual meeting of the American Educational Research Association, San Diego, CA.

City, E. A., Elmore, R. F., Fiarman, S. E., & Teitel, L. (2009). *Instructional rounds in education: A network approach to improving teaching and learning.* Cambridge, MA: Harvard Education Press.

Coles, R., & Ford, G. (2010). *The story of Ruby Bridges.* New York, NY: Scholastic Inc.

Collet, V. S. (2011). *The gradual increase of responsibility: Scaffolds for change* (Unpublished doctoral dissertation). ProQuest UMI Number: 3475305. University at Buffalo, State University of New York, Buffalo, NY.

Collet, V. S. (2017). Lesson Study in a tTurnaround school: Local knowledge as a pressure-balanced valve for improved instruction. *Teachers College Record, 119*(6), 1–58.

Covey, S. (2004). *Seven habits of highly effective people.* New York, NY: Simon & Schuster.

Daly, A. J. (2009). Rigid response in an age of accountability: The potential of leadership and trust. *Educational Administration Quarterly, 45,* 168–216.

Danielson, C. (2011). *Enhancing professional practice: A framework for teaching* (2nd ed.). Alexandria, VA: Association for Supervision and Curriculum Development.

Danielson, C. (2015). *Talk about teaching! Leading professional conversations.* Thousand Oaks, CA: Corwin Press.

Darling-Hammond, L., Hyler, M. E., & Gardner, M. (2017). *Effective teacher professional development.* Palo Alto, CA: Learning Policy Institute.

Davis, J. (2001). American Indian boarding school experiences: Recent studies from Native perspectives. *OAH Magazine of History, 15*(2), 20–22. Retrieved from https://www.jstor.org/stable/25163421?seq=1#metadata_info_tab_contents

Dolton, P., & Marcenaro-Gutierrez, O. (2013). Varkey Gems Foundation 2013 global teacher status index. Retrieved from https://www.varkeyfoundation.org/sites/default/files/documents/2013GlobalTeacherStatusIndex.pdf

Duckworth, A. (2016). *Grit: The power of passion and perseverance.* New York, NY: Simon & Schuster.

Dudley, P. (2012). Lesson Study development in England: From school networks to national policy. *International Journal for Lesson and Learning Studies, 1*(1), 86–100.

DuFour, R. (2004). Leading edge: The best staff development is in the workplace, not in a workshop. *Journal of Staff Development, 25*(2), 63–64.

DuFour, R., & Marzano, R. J. (2011). *Leaders of learning: How district, school, and classroom leaders improve student achievement.* Bloomington, IN: Solution Tree Press.

Fenwick, L., & Cooper, M. (2013). Learning about the effects of context on teaching and learning in pre-service teacher education. *Australian Journal of Teacher Education, 38*(3), 96–110.

Fontichiaro, K. (2010). Cross curriculum: Awakening and building prior knowledge with Primary Sources: See, think, wonder. *School Library Monthly, 27*(1), 14–15.

Franke, M. L., Carpenter, T. P., Levi, L., & Fennema, E. (2001). Capturing teachers' generative change: A follow-up study of professional development in mathematics. *American Educational Research Journal, 38*(3), 653–689.

Fullan, M. (2007). Change the terms for teacher learning. *Journal of Staff Development, 28*(3), 35–36.

Gallagher, K. (2015). *In the best interest of students: Staying true to what works in the ELA classroom.* Portland, ME: Stenhouse Publishers.

Garcia, A., & O'Donnell-Allen, C. (2015). *Pose, wobble, flow: A culturally proactive approach to literacy instruction.* New York, NY: Teachers College Press.

Gay, G. (2010). *Culturally relevant teaching* (2nd ed.). New York, NY: Teachers College Press.

Gersten, R., Taylor, M. J., Keys, T. D., Rolfhus, E., & Newman-Gonchar, R. (2014). *Summary of research on the effectiveness of math professional development approaches* (REL 2014–010). Washington, DC: U.S. Department of Education, Institute of Education Sciences, National Center for Education Evaluation and Regional Assistance, Regional Educational Laboratory Southeast.

González, N., Moll, L. C., & Amanti, C. (Eds.). (2006). *Funds of knowledge: Theorizing practices in households, communities, and classrooms.* New York, NY: Routledge.

Guskey, T. R. (2005). Taking a second look at accountability: Strong evidence reflecting the benefits of professional development is more important than ever before. *Journal of Staff Development, 26*(1), 10–18.

Gutiérrez, K. D., & Penuel, W. R. (2014). Relevance to practice as a criterion for rigor. *Educational Researcher, 43*(1), 19–23.

Hanford, E. (2015). A different approach to teacher learning: Lesson study. *America Radio Works.* Retrieved from http://www.americanradioworks.org/segments/a-different-approach-to-teacher-learning-lesson-study/

Harn, B., Parisi, D., & Stoolmiller, M. (2013). Balancing fidelity with flexibility and fit: What do we really know about fidelity implementation in schools. *Exceptional Children, 79*(2), 181–193.

Harwayne, S. (2000). *Lifetime guarantees.* Portsmouth, NH: Heinemann.

Hassett, D. D. (2008). Teacher flexibility and judgment: A multidynamic literacy theory. *Journal of Early Childhood Literacy, 8*(3), 295–327.

Hattie, J. (2012). *Visible learning for teachers: Maximizing impact on learning.* New York, NY: Routledge.

He, Y. (2009). Strength-based mentoring in pre-service teacher education: A literature review. *Mentoring & Tutoring: Partnership in Learning, 17*(3), 263–275.

Heineke, A. J., & McTighe, J. (2018). *Using understanding by design in the culturally and linguistically diverse classroom.* Alexandria, VA: ASCD.

Higgins, J., & Parsons, R. (2009). A successful professional development model in mathematics: A system-wide New Zealand case. *Journal of Teacher Education, 60*(3), 231–242.

Holm, T. (2005). *The great confusion in Indian affairs: Native Americans and whites in the Progressive Era.* Austin, TX: University of Texas Press.

Honigsfeld, A., & Cohan, A. (2008). The power of two. *Journal of Staff Development, 29*(1), 24–28.

Horn, I. S., & Little, J. W. (2010). Attending to problems of practice: routines and resources for professional learning in teachers' workplace interactions. *American Educational Research Journal, 47*(1), 181–217.

Howard, T. C., & Rodriguez-Minkoff, A. (2017). Culturally relevant pedagogy 20 years later: Progress or pontificating? What have we learned, and where do we go? *Teachers College Record, 119*(1), 1–32.

Hurd, J., & Licciardo-Musso, L. (2005). Lesson study: Teacher-led professional development in literacy instruction. *Language Arts, 82*(5), 388–395.

Johnson, C. C., & Fargo, J. D. (2014). A study of the impact of transformative professional development on Hispanic student performance on state mandated assessments of science in elementary school. *Journal of Elementary Science Teacher Education, 25*(7), 845–859.

Johnston, P. H. (2004). *Choice words: How our language affects children's learning.* York, ME: Stenhouse Publishers.

Johnstone, B. (2008). *Discourse analysis.* Malden, MA: Blackwell.

Kabat-Zinn, J. (2003). Mindfulness-based interventions in context: Past, present, and future. *Clinical Psychology: Science and Practice, 10*, 144–156.

Kamii, C., & Russell, K. A. (2012). Elapsed time: Why is it so difficult to teach? *Journal for Research in Mathematics Education, 43*(3), 296–315.

Keene, E. O. (2008). *To understand: New horizons in reading comprehension.* Portsmouth, NH: Heinemann.

Kierkegaard, S. (1843). *The journals of Søren Kierkegaard, Journal IV A* (unpublished). Retrieved from https://en.wikiquote.org/wiki/S%C3%B8ren_Kierkegaard

Kolb, D. (1984). *Experiential learning: Experience as the source of learning and development.* Englewood Cliffs, NJ: Prentice Hall.

Leikin, R., & Dinur, S. (2007). Teacher flexibility in mathematics. *Journal of Mathematical Behavior, 26*, 328–347.

Lewis, C. (2015) What is improvement science? Do we need it in education? *Educational Researcher, 44*(1), 54–61.

Lewis, C., & Hurd, J. (2011). *Lesson Study step by step: How teacher learning communities improve instruction.* Portsmouth, NH: Heinemann.

Lewis, C., & Perry, R. (2014). Lesson Study with mathematical resources: A sustainable model for locally-led teacher professional learning. *Mathematics Teacher Education and Development, 16*(1).

Lewis, C. C., Perry, R. R., Friedkin, S., & Roth, J. R. (2012). Improving teaching does improve teachers: Evidence from Lesson Study. *Journal of Teacher Education, 63*(5), 368–375.

Lewis, C., Perry, R., Hurd, J., & O'Connell, M. (2006). Lesson Study comes of age in North America. *Phi Delta Kappan, 88*(4), 273–81.

Lewis, C., Perry, R., & Murata, A. (2006). How should research contribute to instructional improvement: The case of lesson study. *Educational Researcher, 35*(3), 3–14.

Lewis, C., & Tsuchida, I. (1998). The basics in Japan: The three C's. *Educational Leadership, 55* (6), 32–37.

Lieberman, A., & Pointer Mace, D. (2010). Making practice public: Teacher learning in the 21st century. *Journal of Teacher Education, 61*(1), 77–88.

Lieberman, A., & Wood, D. R. (2002). The National Writing Project. *Educational Leadership, 59*(6), 40–44.

Little, J. W. (1982). Norms of collegiality and experimentation: Workplace conditions of school success. *American Educational Research Journal, 19*(3), 325–340.

Lizárraga, J. R., & Gutiérrez, K. D. (2018). Centering Nepantla literacies from the borderlands: Leveraging "in-betweenness" toward learning in the everyday. *Theory into Practice, 57*(1), 38–47.

Lortie, D. (1975). *Schoolteacher: A sociological study.* Chicago, IL: University of Chicago Press.

Lovell, P., & Catrow, D. (2011). *Stand tall, Molly Lou Melon.* London, UK: Penguin.

Lucas, L. (2017). *Practicing presence: Simple self-care strategies for teachers.* Portland, ME: Stenhouse.

Luke, A. (2016, December). LRA 2016 distinguished scholar lifetime achievement session. Literacy Research Association. 2016 Literacy Research Association Annual Conference. Retrieved from https://www.youtube.com/watch?v=swWWWlZOqPg&

Maggio, R. (1992). *The Beacon book of quotations by women.* Boston, MA: Beacon Press.

Maloch, B. (2002). Scaffolding student talk: One teacher's role in literature discussion groups. *Reading Research Quarterly, 37*(1), 94–112.

Marble, S. (2007). Inquiring into teaching: Lesson study in elementary science methods. *Journal of Science Teacher Education, 18*(6), 935–953.

Mariconda, B., & Aurey, D. (2005). *The comprehensive expository writing guide* (2nd ed.). Monroe, CT: Empowering Writers.

Marrongelle, K., Sztajn, P., & Smith, M. (2013). Scaling up professional development in an era of common state standards. *Journal of Teacher Education, 64,* 202–211.

Matanzo, J. B., & Harris, D. L. (1999). Encouraging metacognitive awareness in preservice literacy courses. *Yearbook of the College Reading Association, 21,* 201–225.

Meehan, R. J. (2011). *The teacher's journey.* Retrieved from http://robertjohnmeehan. blogspot.com/

Merriam, E. (2005). A lazy thought. In S. James (Ed.), *Days like this: A collection of small poems,* (p. 10). Somerville, MA: Candlewick Press.

Miller, D., Topping, K., & Thurston, A. (2010). Peer tutoring in reading: The effects of role and organization on two dimensions of self-esteem. *British Journal of Educational Psychology, 80*(3), 417-433.

Moll, L. C., Amanti, C., Neff, D., & González, N. (2006). Funds of knowledge for teaching: Using a qualitative approach to connect homes and classrooms. *Theory into Practice, 31*(2), 132–144.

Moolenaar, N. M., Sleegers, P. J., & Daly, A. J. (2012). Teaming up: Linking collaboration networks, collective efficacy, and student achievement. *Teaching and Teacher Education, 28*(2), 251–262.

Murray, D. (1996). Rewriting teaching. In B. M. Powers & R. S. Hubbard, *Oops: What we learn when our teaching fails* (pp. 47–49). York, ME: Stenhouse.

National Union of Teachers. (n.d.). *Valuing teachers, valuing education.* Chelmsford, UK: Ruskin Press. Retrieved from https://www.teachers.org.uk/files/valuing-teachers—8487-.pdf

National Writing Project. (2018, January 25). *Unpacking the NWP social practices framework: Going public with our practice.* Retrieved from https://www.nwp.org/cs/public/print/resource/4719

Newkirk, T. (2017). *Embarrassment: And the emotional underlife of learning.* Portsmouth, NH: Heinemann.

Park, H. (2015). *The eight answers for happiness.* Bloomington, IN: Xlibris.

Patterson, A., & Tolnay, T. (2015). Bringing teacher learning to life: Courageous teaching using peer learning labs to elevate efficacy. Retrieved from https://www.pebc.org/wp-content/uploads/2016/07/PeerLearningLabs_web.pdf

Perry, R. R., & Lewis, C. C. (2009). What is successful adaptation of lesson study in the US? *Journal of Educational Change, 10*(4), 365–391.

Pesick, S. (2005). "Lesson Study" and the teaching of American history: Connecting professional development and classroom practice. *Social Studies Review, 44*(2), 43–60.

Plank, S. B., & Condliffe, B. F. (2013). Pressures of the season: An examination of classroom quality and high-stakes accountability. *American Educational Research Journal, 50*(5), 1152–1182.

Pomerance, B. (1977). *The elephant man.* New York, NY: Grove Press.

Prater, M. A., & Devereaux, T. H. (2009). Culturally responsive training of teacher educators. *Action in Teacher Education, 31*(3), 19–27.

Priestley, M., Edwards, R., Priestley, A., & Miller, K. (2012). Teacher agency in curriculum making: Agents of change and spaces for manoeuvre. *Curriculum Inquiry, 42*(2), 191–214.

Proust, M. (1974). *La Prisonnière: A la recherche du temps perdu* (Vol. 5). Paris, France: Gallimard.

Puchner, L. D., & Taylor, A. R. (2006). Lesson study, collaboration and teacher efficacy: Stories from two school-based math lesson study groups. *Teaching and Teacher Education, 22*(7), 922–934.

Rosenblatt, Z. (2004). Skill flexibility and school change: A multi-national study. *Journal of Educational Change, 5,* 1–30.

Rosenow, N. (2012). *Heart-centered teaching inspired by nature: Using nature's wisdom to bring more joy and effectiveness to our work with children.* Lincoln, NE: Dimensions Educational Research Foundation.

Rother, M. (2009). *Toyota kata.* New York, NY: McGraw-Hill Professional Publishing.

Rovenstine, J. (2012). "Oggy Oggy Oggy" [Giclee print]. Retrieved from https://www.etsy.com/listing/105912929/12-x-12-giclee-print-oggy-oggy-oggy-2012

Rumelhart, D. E., & Norman, D. A. (1976). *Accretion, tuning and restructuring: Three modes of learning* (No. 7602). California University, La Jolla Center for Human Information Processing.

Rust, F. (2009). Teacher research and the problem of practice. *Teachers College Record, 111*(8), 1882–1893.

Sagor, R. (2000). *Guiding school improvement with action research.* Alexandria, VA: Association for Supervision and Curriculum Development.

Schlechty, P. C. (1990). *Schools for the 21st century: Leadership imperatives of educational reform.* San Francisco, CA: Jossey-Bass.

Schlechty, P. C. (2002). *Working on the work: An action plan for teachers, principals, and superintendents.* San Francisco, CA: Jossey-Bass.

Schön, D. A. (1987). *Educating the reflective practitioner.* San Francisco, CA: Jossey-Bass.

Senge, P. (1990) *The fifth discipline: The art and practice of the learning organization.* New York, NY: Currency.

Senn, N. (2012). Effective approaches to motivate and engage reluctant boys in literacy. *The Reading Teacher, 66*(3), 211–220.

Shuck, B., Reio Jr., T. G., & Rocco, T. S. (2011). Employee engagement: An examination of antecedent and outcome variables. *Human resource development international, 14*(4), 427–445.

Shulman, L. S. (1986). Those who understand: Knowledge growth in teaching. *Educational Researcher, 15*(2), 4–14.

Sibbald, T. (2009). The relationship between lesson study and self-efficacy. *School Science and Mathematics, 109*(8), 450–460.

Smit, J., & van Eerde, D. (2013). What counts as evidence for the long-term realization of whole-class scaffolding? *Learning, Culture, and Social Interaction, 2*(1), 22–31.

Smith, M. S., Hughes, E. K., Engle, R. A., & Stein, M. K. (2009). Orchestrating discussions of challenging tasks: Keeping your eye on the mathematics to be learned. *Mathematics Teaching in the Middle School, 14*(9), 548–556.

Snicket, L. (2007). *The latke who couldn't stop screaming: A Christmas story.* San Francisco, CA: McSweeney's Books.

Soto, G., & Martinez, E. (1996). *Too many tamales.* London, UK: Penguin.

Spillane, J. P., Parise, L. M., & Sherer, J. Z. (2011). Organizational routines as coupling mechanisms: Policy, school administration, and the technical core. *American Educational Research Journal, 48*(3), 586–619.

Spiro, R. J., Collins, B. P., & Ramchandran, A. (2007). Reflections on a post-Gutenberg epistemology for video use in ill-structured domains: Fostering complex learning and cognitive flexibility. In R. Goldman, R. Pea, B. Barron, & S. Derry (Eds.), *Video research in the learning sciences* (pp. 93–100). Mahwah, NJ: Lawrence Erlbaum Associates.

Spiro, R. J., & Jehng, J. C. (1990). Cognitive flexibility and hypertext: Theory and technology for the nonlinear and multidimensional traversal of complex subject matter. In D. Nix & R. Spiro (Eds.), *Cognition, education, and multimedia: Exploring ideas in high technology* (pp. 163–205). Hillsdale, NJ: Lawrence Erlbaum Associates.

Staw, B. M., Sandelands, L. E., & Dutton, J. E. (1981). Threat rigidity effects in organizational behavior: A multilevel analysis. *Administrative Science Quarterly*, 501–524.

Stigler, J. W., & Hiebert, J. (1999). *The teaching gap: Best ideas from the world's teachers for improving education in the classroom.* New York, NY: Free Press.

Strawser, J. (2009, May/June). Writing rapture. *Writer's Digest, 89*(3), 48.

Strong, R., Silver, H. F., & Robinson, A. (1995). What do students want (and what really motivates them)? *Educational Leadership, 53*(1), 8–12.

Surowiecki, J. (2005). *The wisdom of crowds.* New York, NY: Anchor.

Takahashi, A., Watanabe, T., Yoshida, M., & Wang-Iverson, P. (2005). Improving content and pedagogical knowledge through Kyozaikenkyu. *In building our understanding of lesson study* (pp. 101–110). Philadelphia, PA: Research for Better Schools, Inc.

Thoonen, E. E., Sleegers, P. J., Oort, F. J., Peetsma, T. T., & Geijsel, F. P. (2011). How to improve teaching practices: The role of teacher motivation, organizational factors, and leadership practices. *Educational Administration Quarterly, 47*(3), 496–536.

U.S. Department of Education. (2016). The state of racial diversity in the educator workforce. Retrieved from https://www2.ed.gov/rschstat/eval/highered/racial-diversity/state-racial-diversity-workforce.pdf

Vacca, R. T., & Vacca, J. L. (2008). *Content area reading.* Boston, MA: Pearson.

Valli, L., & Buese, D. (2007). The changing roles of teachers in an era of high-stakes accountability. *American Educational Research Journal, 44*(3), 519–558.

Vygotsky, L. S. (1978). *Mind in society: The development of higher psychological processes.* Cambridge, MA: Harvard University Press.

Vygotsky, L. S. (2012). *Thought and language.* Cambridge, MA: MIT Press.

Waldron, N. L., & McLeskey, J. (2010). Establishing a collaborative school culture through comprehensive school reform. *Journal of Educational and Psychological Consultation, 20*(1), 58–74.

Wardlow, L. (2016). *The science behind student engagement.* Boston, MA: Pearson.

Wei, R. C., Darling-Hammond, L., & Adamson, F. (2010). *Professional development in the United States: Trends and challenges* (Vol. 28). Dallas, TX: National Staff Development Council.

Whitcomb, J., Borko, H., & Liston, D. (2009). Growing talent: Promising professional development models and practices. *Journal of Teacher Education, 60*(3), 207–212.

Wieble, S., Lyle, E., Wright, P. R., Dark, K., McLarnon, M., & Day, L. (Eds.). (2017). *Ways of being in teaching: Conversations and reflections.* Boston, MA: Sense Publishers.

Wiggins, G. P., & McTighe, J. (2005). *The understanding by design guide to creating high-quality units.* Alexandria, VA: ASCD.

Yoon, K. S., Duncan, T., Lee, S. W.-Y., Scarloss, B., & Shapley, K. (2007). *Reviewing the evidence on how teacher professional development affects student achievement* (Issues & Answers Report, REL 2007—No. 033). Washington, DC: U.S. Department of Education, Institute of Education Sciences, National Center for Education Evaluation and Regional Assistance, Regional Educational Laboratory Southwest.

Index

Note: Page numbers followed by f refer to illustrations.

About the Author

Vicki S. Collet is an associate professor in the Department of Curriculum and Instruction at the University of Arkansas. Prior to becoming a teacher educator, she worked as a district curriculum coordinator, instructional coach, interventionist, and elementary and secondary classroom teacher.